Assertiveness Training

Mastering Assertive Communication to Learn How to be Yourself and Still Manage to Win the Respect of Others.

ZAC M. CRUZ

ASSERTIVENESS TRAINING

© COPYRIGHT 2019 – ZAC M. CRUZ- ALL RIGHTS RESERVED.

This document is geared towards providing exact and reliable information in regards to the topic and issue covered. The publication is sold with the idea that the publisher is not required to render accounting, officially permitted, or otherwise, qualified services. If advice is necessary, legal or professional, a practiced individual in the profession should be ordered.

- From a Declaration of Principles which was accepted and approved equally by a Committee of the American Bar Association and a Committee of Publishers and Associations.

In no way is it legal to reproduce, duplicate, or transmit any part of this document in either electronic means or in printed format. Recording of this publication is strictly prohibited and any storage of this document is not allowed unless with written permission from the publisher. All rights reserved.

ASSERTIVENESS TRAINING

The information provided herein is stated to be truthful and consistent, in that any liability, in terms of inattention or otherwise, by any usage or abuse of any policies, processes, or directions contained within is the solitary and utter responsibility of the recipient reader. Under no circumstances will any legal responsibility or blame be held against the publisher for any reparation, damages, or monetary loss due to the information herein, either directly or indirectly.

Respective authors own all copyrights not held by the publisher.

The information herein is offered for informational purposes solely, and is universal as so. The presentation of the information is without contract or any type of guarantee assurance.

The trademarks that are used are without any consent, and the publication of the trademark is without permission or backing by the trademark owner.

ASSERTIVENESS TRAINING

All trademarks and brands within this book are for clarifying purposes only and are the owned by the owners themselves, not affiliated with this document.

ASSERTIVENESS TRAINING

ASSERTIVENESS TRAINING

TABLE OF CONTENTS

INTRODUCTION 8

CHAPTER 1: UNDERSTANDING ASSERTIVENESS 13

CHAPTER 2: DEVELOPING ASSERTIVE BODY LANGUAGE 43

CHAPTER 3: THE ASSERTIVENESS BOOT CAMP 57

CHAPTER 4: ASSERTIVENESS IN THE WORKPLACE 84

CHAPTER 5: ASSERTIVENESS FOR WOMEN 134

CHAPTER 6: ASSERTIVENESS IN RELATIONSHIPS 153

CHAPTER 7: DEALING WITH HOSTILITY AND MANIPULATION.. 174

CHAPTER 8: ASSERTIVENESS IS A CHOICE 191

CONCLUSION 211

Introduction

It's good that others think of you as a nice person, right? Being nice means that others will see you as a caring, gentle soul that would never do them any wrong. It also means that you put yourself last and prioritize the happiness of others before yours. If you are nice, people will know you for being easy-going and avoiding conflict at all cost. Because of this, it only makes sense that you'd be happier being non-confrontational in the long-term.

Sadly, quite the opposite is right in the majority of cases: people that try the hardest to be nice to others tend to end up feeling the most miserable and frustrated. They also have very levels of low self-esteem and confidence to boot. There is a dark truth about being a nice person: it rarely comes out of having high morals or pure kindness.

ASSERTIVENESS TRAINING

In reality, nice people are driven by the constant fear of displeasing others and receiving their disapproval.

A few years ago, if you'd asked my friends and family to describe me, "Assertive" wouldn't be one of the adjectives they would have used. I was deeply aware of this fact, and it just left me feeling more miserable until I finally mustered up the courage to get this and several other related areas of my life handled for good. Although I wasn't known as being a super nice guy, I rarely spoke up my mind, had a tough time saying no to most requests, and when I disagreed with something or someone I secretly wished I dared to voice my opinion. My overall sense of self-worth was deficient. Most people would've described me as your average shy introvert.

Several times per week, I had to bottle up my opinions and thoughts because of how difficult it was for me to let others know what I was honestly thinking. Of course, this led to a lot of frustration and further affected the low self-esteem I had.

ASSERTIVENESS TRAINING

If you have a difficult time saying no to others, reserve your opinions to yourself, and continuously put other's needs above your own, people will become aware of this fact and will start to expect this type of special treatment and behaviors from you at all times. At some point, you'll inevitably feel burnt out from other's expectations, and you'll feel resentful for not being able to act from the point of authenticity.

Whenever I saw someone speak up their minds, and often get what they wanted, I secretly wished I dared to do the same. I started to question if they had specific personality traits that made it so easy for them to be so vocal about their thoughts. After all, I was an introvert, and introverts are supposed to be shy and quiet, right?...

Most tend to believe the false paradigm that people are born a certain way – for instance; you are either charismatic or you aren't. You are a passive person or you're an aggressive one.

But in reality, there are several attributes that we can develop by consciously modifying our behaviors through constant practice. It took me a while to realize that this is possible. The thought of being an introvert that wasn't shy or afraid of speaking his mind clashed profoundly with what I had been taught.

It's not easy to break out of the niceness walls, especially after years of behaving too nice and having the people that surround you to expect you to act a certain way.

This guide will help you understand how to find the right balance between being too nice and being aggressive so that you can naturally let go of old paradigms that are holding you back from expressing your authentic self.

Acting this way will prevent you from feeling resentment or guilt towards the actions and decisions you make.

ASSERTIVENESS TRAINING

The benefits of being more assertive can be quite profound and will be explored in-depth in the following chapters. I hope that by the end of the book you will feel empowered to speak out and stand up for yourself in a respectful way that leads to an improved quality of life and better long term-happiness, just as it did for me after putting in the work.

If you expect this book to be full of "hacks" or be a magic bullet remedy for shyness, you'll be severely disappointed. Creating a stronger identity that is in line with your core values and beliefs and being able to speak up your mind without feeling remorse or second thoughts is not something that happens overnight. It requires a commitment and effort, but the life benefits will be everlasting and profound.

Thank you, and I hope you enjoy this guide. If you'd like to support the work of independent authors, the only thing I ask is if you could please leave a review after reading this book.

CHAPTER 1: UNDERSTANDING ASSERTIVENESS

What is assertiveness?

It's common to hear the phrase, "You need to be more assertive." However, most people misunderstand the term assertiveness, and even fewer people have a good grasp of what it truly means to be assertive. So what exactly is assertiveness? In a few words, assertiveness is a communication style that allows you to express your ideas, emotions, needs, and opinions in a way that prevents you from stepping on the right of others. There are other styles of communication such as aggressive, passive and passive-aggressive that end up either harming either our rights or the rights of others.

An in-depth look at the four main styles of communication:

Passive communication. A communication style where individuals avoid expressing their ideas, needs, and opinions. People that have adopted a passive communication style tend to respond poorly to hurtful or anger-inducing situations, often allowing grievances and annoyances to accumulate slowly, while they go through with their lives, unaware of the build-up. Once their tolerance for unacceptable behavior reaches a specific limit, they often resort to outbursts of rage that tend to be out of proportion with the triggering event. After such outburst, they might feel a lot of guilt and regret, so they quickly go back to a passive form of communication.

Those that adopt a passive style of communication tend to fail to express their needs, ideas, and emotions, often letting others to step on their rights and speak in a soft voice tone while apologizing often.

They also tend to avoid eye contact and have non-verbal communication that makes them look as weak to others. Some people that communicate passively typically speak very softly and apologetically. They might even apologize ahead of time when they say an opinion or negatively qualify their statements.

Most people, including myself, start with a passive style of communication, as it is the most common one adopted by introverts, people with low self-esteem and those that are afraid to speak up.

For instance, this is something that an overly passive person would say– "This might sound to you like a dumb question, but have you tried fixing the issue from this angle?". This constant apologizing and qualifying comes from low self-confidence and a feeling of anxiety about being seen as stubborn or aggressive.

ASSERTIVENESS TRAINING

Having a passive style of communication has several short and long term adverse effects:

-Passive people often feel anxious when interacting with others, since mostly everything feels out of their control.

-They feel depressed and resentful because their needs and wants aren't usually met.

-Their issues tend never to get addressed, slowly piling up and creating more frustration.

-People that have developed a passive style of communication tend to create social anxiety disorders.

ASSERTIVENESS TRAINING

If you can relate to a few of the following statements, then, likely, you're primarily using a passive communication style:

-"Standing up to my rights doesn't come naturally to me."

-"I'm unaware of what my rights are."

-"It's very common for me to feel like I'm either ignored or getting stepped on by others."

-"I don't feel like I'm able to take proper care of myself."

-"I feel like others do not value me enough".

Aggressive communication. This style of communication is the other opposite end of the spectrum. People that use an aggressive form of communication are often able to express their ideas, needs, and emotions; however, they do so by rarely considering and respecting the rights of others. If you use an aggressive communication style, your interests are often the main priority, even if this means that you'll step on others to get what you want or use forceful communication to shutdown contrasting opinions and ideas.

Aggressive communicators tend to use a lot of accusatory "you" statements and attack others instead of attempting to do a neutral expression of their needs. For instance, saying things such as "you always talk too fast" or "you are a very reckless driver."

I remember that at first, I often looked up to people that used an aggressive style of communication. After all, I thought, they seemed to get what they wanted.

ASSERTIVENESS TRAINING

We will

Those that are in positions of power, such as managers, team leaders, and bosses that communicate using an aggressive style make others think of them as inflexible, selfish and demanding.

Aggressive communicators often will:

-Use manipulation and humiliation tactics to control others.

-Act on impulse.

-Use a lot of accusatory "you" statements.

-Interrupt others frequently.

-Be poor listeners.

-Try to dominate others.

-Speak in a bossy and demanding voice.

-Rarely ask questions, as they are not interested in others' needs and ideas.

-Be unable to make compromises.

If you can relate to the following statements, then you are probably using an aggressive style of communication:

-"I feel like my ideas and needs are more important than those of others."

-"Whenever I'm negotiating, I try to look for the outcome that best benefits me."

-"I like to blame others and make them feel bad about their mistakes."

-"I tend to be impulsive and react fairly fast."

-"I'm often perceived as loud or bossy by others."

-"Others often say that I have a huge sense of entitlement."

Passive-aggressive communication. This third style of communication tends not to be as well-known as the other three. It is a combination of the first two styles.

ASSERTIVENESS TRAINING

However, it is often used by individuals that want to appear as passive on the surface but are acting out their anger in subtle or indirect ways. Those that have developed a passive-aggressive style of communication often feel the same way as passive communicators do; they feel powerless, frustrated and resentful since they feel like they are not able to deal directly with their issues or the cause of their frustrations. They tend to express their anger very subtly, often by undermining what they believe is causing their resentment.

Passive communicators tend not to speak their message directly and instead convey it through ambiguous actions or disrespectful or annoying comments.

Passive-aggressive communicators often will:

-Have a hard time acknowledging their anger.

ASSERTIVENESS TRAINING

-Use sarcasm liberally.

-Deny there is an issue.

-Have a cooperative image while purposely doing disruptive things.

-Act out in subtle or indirect manners.

-Use non-verbal communication that is not consistent with the way they feel. (For instance, smiling when they're upset about something).

If you can relate to the following statements, then you are probably using a passive-aggressive communication style:

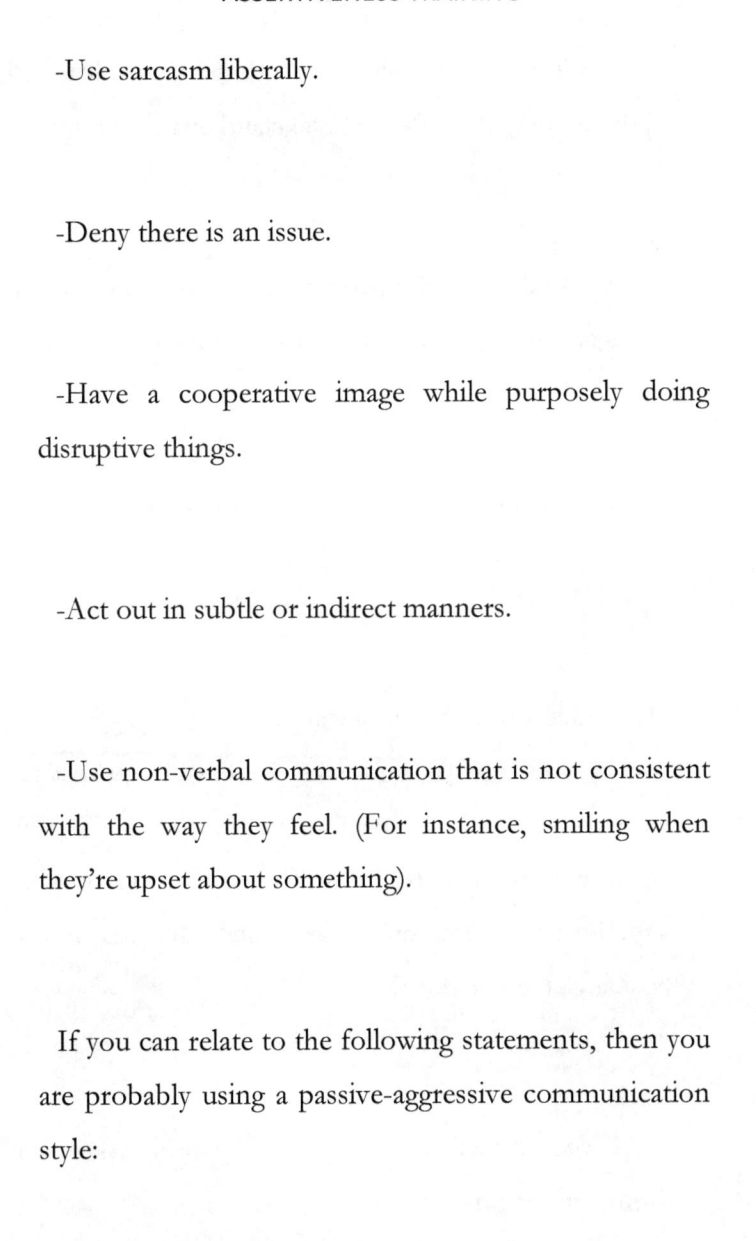

-"I don't feel like I'm able to stand up for my ideas and needs, so instead, I often sabotage and disrupt others."

-"I dislike dealing with people directly, and prefer using tactics and strategies to get what I want instead."

-"I often appear to be cooperative, when, in reality, I'm not."

The first three communication styles – aggressive, passive, and passive-aggressive are flawed approaches that have more disadvantages than advantages. They all tend to elicit negative responses from others too. So what is the best overall communication style that fits best in most social interactions?

Yep, you've probably guessed it by now: **Assertive communication.**

ASSERTIVENESS TRAINING

Individuals that use this style of communication can clearly state their needs, opinions, and feelings while firmly advocating for their rights and obligations without disrupting or violating others. These individuals, not only value their emotions, time and needs, but they also prioritize being respectful to the rights of others. While no style of communication can guarantee positive reactions, assertive communication tends to be the most effective in the long run.

Assertive communicators often will:

-State their ideas, needs, and emotions clearly and respectfully.

-Use "I" statements instead of "you" statements.

-Rarely feel like they don't have any control or say in a situation.

-Have an easier time connecting with others.

-Have good, well-calibrated eye contact.

-Speak in a very calm and clear tone of voice.

-Be very respectful of others.

If you can relate to the following statements, then you are probably using an assertive communication style:

-"I like to speak honestly and direct to the point."

-"I feel like I bring a lot of value to others."

-"I'm aware that I have choices in my life and that a lot is in my own hands."

-"It's better to control oneself instead of trying to control others."

-"Having my rights respected is one of my biggest priorities."

-"Most of my happiness is in my control."

-"I respect the rights of others as much as I do mine."

It's not difficult to see how an assertive style of communication can help us take care of ourselves, have better mental health, and build stronger relationships.

Common myths about assertiveness

Since people often misunderstand assertiveness, lots of misconceptions surround it. Many individuals that use the other three styles of communication tend to use these as an excuse for why they shouldn't try to be more assertive.

Let's take a look at some of the most common ways of thinking that might be preventing us from being assertive and then what we can do to change them.

Myth: There is not much difference between assertiveness and aggressiveness.

Reality: A lot of people that use an aggressive style of communication believe that they are assertive simply because they can state what their needs are to others.

While it is true that the ability to effectively communicate your needs is present in both aggressive and assertive styles of communication, there are significant differences between doing so in either stating them assertively or aggressively. For instance, there are differences in the choice of words, tone of voice and body language used between both.

Myth: By being assertive, I will get what I want.

Reality: Using an assertive style of communication doesn't mean that you will always be able to get what you want. Being assertive is not a guarantee of any outcome you desire. However, by acting assertively, what you'll tend to get is a positive response from others, and often, the best possible response in that situation. Because assertiveness is all about being able to express yourself in a way that respects not only your needs but those of others, you'll sometimes be able to get what you want, but sometimes this simply won't be possible.

However, you'll more often be able to meet at a mutually satisfactory point with others whenever you can't fully get what you want.

Myth: One has to change their core self to become assertive.

Reality: This is a common myth that is entirely false. Assertiveness isn't about changing who you are, but instead, is all about helping you communicate and relate more effectively with others. Assertive people know their rights and prioritize their needs, but they understand where their boundaries tend to be and can make them clear to others.

Myth: There's no need to be assertive with friends and family.

Reality: Unfortunately, not even your friends and family can read your mind, even if it might seem that way to you from time to time. So for them to understand how we're feeling and what our needs are, we have to communicate clearly with them or it's likely that they'll never know about our needs. Simple as that.

Myth: Being mostly passive is the best way to be loved by most people.

Reality: This is false. Those that use a passive communication style are always agreeing with others and letting them get their way, while their individual needs and emotions get stepped over. By being passive, you give in to their needs without prioritizing yours and making requests of your own. This style of behavior rarely makes others respect or admire you.

The opposite tends to happen as people will see you as dull or lacking character and can quickly grow frustrated with their inability to be able to connect with you.

Myth: If I start acting assertive, I will have to be assertive in every situation.

Reality: Understanding how to communicate assertively will give you a lot of freedom and choices. You will be able to decide when to be assertive and when not to be. Although an assertive style of communication tends to be the best approach for most situations, there are several instances when it might not the most helpful way to proceed. For example, imagine that you are dealing with a physically violent person that is acting aggressively. Interacting assertively with them might put you at risk, as the person is not acting rationally at that moment. In situations like these, a passive approach might manage to get a better outcome

ASSERTIVENESS TRAINING

The adverse effects of not being assertive

There are several side effects of not being assertive, the main one being the development of a low sense of self-worth. When you communicate passively, you are hiding away what you think or feel. Because of this, you'll end up agreeing with things that you don't like and prioritize other people's needs instead of your own. Doing this often leads to a feeling of having little no control over your life.

If you never express yourself openly and often conceal your ideas and emotions, you will feel tense, frustrated, anxious, and even resentful. It can also lead to a lot of issues in relationships. It's not nice when you feel like even your friends and family don't know you.

If on the other hand, we continue to communicate aggressively, we will eventually start losing our friends and the respect of others. Surprisingly, a lot of people that communicate aggressively tend to have low self-esteem. On the other hand, people behave more assertively tend to feel less depressed and have better health outcomes. Less assertive people tend to suffer from more mood disorders and phobias.

Are people born assertive?

A common question is whether we are born or become assertive through learned behaviors. The truth is that we are all born assertive. Think about how a baby cries whenever they want something. They feel entirely free to express their emotions and needs. As they grow, they start to adapt their behavior to better fit in with the responses received from their environment. Their actions become influenced by the reactions they receive from their family members, peers, authority figures, etc.

ASSERTIVENESS TRAINING

If a child grows up in an environment where their parents tend to deal with conflict through constant arguing and yelling, then they might learn to deal with conflict in a similar way. Over time, the child might develop an aggressive style of communication. On the other hand, if a child is taught to put other's needs before their own and to try to please others, they will find it harder to be assertive. In some cases, family or peers might tell them to try not to express "negative" emotions, or else they might be ridiculed or seen as odd; as a result, the child learns quickly not to show any "negative" feelings.

If you'd like to understand better why you don't communicate assertively, you could try answering the following questions:

-How did my family and peers handle conflict?

ASSERTIVENESS TRAINING

-What actions did they take whenever they disagreed with someone?

-How did my parents teach me to deal with difficult situations such as conflict?

-How did they teach me to get what I want without having to ask directly?

-Do I still find myself using these methods to get what you want?

These are often strong reasons why we become unassertive as we develop. Children and teenagers learn to adapt their behaviors in a way that works best for them at the time. For instance, if you tried being assertive with parents or peers that used an aggressive communication style and it got you into trouble, you might have learned that it's better to stay under the radar instead.

Or if you had a rough childhood, you may have realized that it's necessary to be aggressive to survive. And it's also very possible that the family members and peers that you learned those behaviors from similarly learned theirs – from someone else.

You mustn't start blaming yourself or others for your lack of assertiveness. It's better to break the cycle and learn how to adopt a new way of behaving and communicating. The good news is that you will not pass on negative ways of behaving to your own family and peers.

What prevents us from being assertive?

There are several reasons why we might not be assertive. We tend to develop these while growing and learning which behaviors helped us get by.

The most common are:

Limiting beliefs. Passive or aggressive people often have unrealistic beliefs and have negative preconceptions about assertiveness. These unrealistic beliefs and assumptions are probably the number one factor why most people tend not to act assertively. In my case, limiting beliefs was perhaps the most significant obstacle I faced throughout this journey.

Some examples of limiting beliefs are:

-If I start acting assertively, I might ruin the relationship I have with my friends.

-It is selfish to state what I want.

-I'm afraid to embarrass myself if I say what I think.

Lacking the right skill set. Some people may already be aware that assertive communication tends to be the most ideal in several cases, but they might not have the necessary verbal or nonverbal skills to do so effectively. If this sounds familiar to you, you may observe other people and admire their behavior, but have no idea of how to carry yourself assertively. This guide will cover most of the right skills that you need to use an assertive communication style correctly.

Lacking social calibration. Another factor might be that you are currently unable to know when you need to use assertive behaviors in specific situations. Some common mistakes made when evaluating situations are mistaking firm assertion with aggression or non-assertion with politeness.

Cultural factors. There can be strong cultural factors that influence your behavior and may be working against you.

For instance, there are some cultures where assertiveness is not as well regarded as it is in others, such as a lot of Western countries. People from such cultures might have a harder time transitioning into a more assertive communication style. The same applies to people raised in a different time. For instance, men from older generations were taught from very early on that expressing their emotions was a sign of weakness, while women were told that stating their needs and opinions was un-ladylike. Deeply rooted beliefs such as these can be tougher to change, but they can definitively be altered.

Assertive rights

When transitioning to a more assertive style of communication, you must understand that everyone has fundamental rights that should be respected at all times. Responding passively means that such rights will be neglected or ignored. On the other hand, reacting aggressively implies that the rights of others can be abused.

ASSERTIVENESS TRAINING

Everyone's assertive rights include:

-The ability to express their needs, ideas, and opinions.

-The ability to make decisions.

-The ability to say "no," "I don't know," or "I don't understand" without feeling bad afterward.

-The ability to be non-assertive if the situation calls for it.

-The ability to change your mind.

-Deciding what you want to do, with your priorities, body, and time.

-The right to make mistakes and be held responsible for them.

CHAPTER 2: DEVELOPING ASSERTIVE BODY LANGUAGE

You might be surprised to hear that the average time that it takes for someone to make an impression on us is not a few minutes or an hour, but a few seconds, and often, its only one. Yes, that's right; it may only take about a single second to make an impression. The following seconds are used to confirm that the initial assessment made was correct.

As social creatures, communication is a massive part of our lives, and 70 to 80 percent of our attention goes to non-verbal communication. In other words, our non-verbals are more critical than the actual words that come out of our mouths (in most cases).

Whenever you're training yourself to become more assertive, remember to place a lot of attention to your body language so that it's corresponding to what you're saying, as congruence is one of the main cornerstones of assertive communication.

Even if you become very skilled at saying the right things at the right time, without the correct use of body language, most of the assertiveness strategies discussed in this guide will pretty much go to waste.

What is non-verbal communication?

Let's start by defining what non-verbal communication is: it is every single communication expression besides the choice of words that you use. Nonverbal communication encompasses your posture, eye movement, breathing, facial expressions, gestures, voice tone, etc. Your mind even has a critical role to play whenever you're interacting with others.

ASSERTIVENESS TRAINING

If you're fearful of a situation or about talking to someone, your mind will inevitably affect the way you express your non-verbal communication. Having a timid or apologetic set of beliefs can fully influence your physiology. As you slowly gain confidence and become more assertive by following the advice in this guide, your mind will gradually become more and more congruent with your non-verbal's and the gap between what you're genuinely feeling and how you're acting will eventually narrow.

Picture for a second someone that is about to be at a job interview; someone who hasn't been employed for a long time and has a lot of debt and other financial problems. If he wants the job very badly and feels very nervous about it, he perhaps will fidget nervously and speak in a hurried tone when being interviewed by his potential employer. If he doesn't pay attention to his non-verbal communication, he will likely make a poor first impression on his interviewer.

ASSERTIVENESS TRAINING

Now imagine that there's a second person who is also interested about the job but knows about how he should carry himself correctly during the interview: he will stand tall and have his shoulders back while speaking slowly. He will also maintain well-calibrated eye contact, neither too much or too little; just enough to make the other person feel at ease.

Learning how to appear and act confident is one of the most useful skills that we can learn in life. Just a small amount of confidence can do wonders for us in several vital situations, from career advancement to negotiating good deals when buying a car or a house. It's easy to understand why: human beings are naturally attracted and influenced by confident people.

So how is it possible to improve your nonverbal communication and genuinely look like you mean what you're saying?

ASSERTIVENESS TRAINING

Developing a good posture

Let's start by developing a good posture, as it is something that can make you immediately appear more confident with little effort. Most people tend to have lousy posture without them noticing. Having poor posture not only makes them look as less confident but may even cause physical issues such as pain in the lower back area. Some people's pain quickly goes away after they make a conscious effort to improve their posture.

Some habits, such as bad posture, can be especially tricky to eliminate. After all, if you've been having poor posture for most of your life, changing this will probably take some consistent, conscious effort from your part. To help you stay on target, you could place little reminders in your car, room or office. A piece of paper with a short note such as "Good posture" should do the trick.

You could also make your phone or computer remind you to be aware of your posture every morning.

How to have good posture:

-Stand up tall. An excellent trick to help you with this is to imagine that you are a marionette that has a string attached to its head. Every time you walk in the room, your puppeteer straightens the string placed in your head, so it's inevitable for you to stand up as tall as you can. Visualization techniques such as this can be incredibly useful to help guide you to the proper position you should be using. When you stand up tall, you'll inevitably feel better (some say they even think slimmer) and more confident.

-Your chin should be kept level with the ground, and your shoulders should be back. The arms should fall naturally at your sides.

ASSERTIVENESS TRAINING

-The feet should be kept about shoulder-width apart. Your weight is best kept on the balls of your feet. Try moving your weight towards your heels and notice how your whole body's tendency will be to slouch with this simple motion. Shifting the load on the balls of your feet does the opposite and helps you maintain good posture.

-Things might fall apart when you start walking, so to help you with this, imagine that you have to balance a book that is on top of your head. If you don't keep both your head and back straight, the book will inevitably fall. Everything else should stay the same when walking, as it is just an extension of standing with good posture.

Extra tips and exercises:

-When sitting down, sit straight as if you were always ready to stand without leaning forward. Keep in mind that your back will probably feel a bit tired at first because you are not used to sitting this way.

ASSERTIVENESS TRAINING

-Place your heels, glutes, and head against a wall. Afterward, pull your shoulder blades back so that they are making contact with the wall too. Try to practice this every day and attempt to increase the length of the stretch in each session.

-Some people find it comfy to recline while they are in the driving seat, but it doesn't do any good for their posture. Instead, it's better to make sure that the seat is close to the steering wheel. Try not to have your legs locked. The knees should be bent slightly. They should be at least at hip level or just slightly above that.

Developing good posture requires straightforward adjustments, but there will be little progress without consistency. If you spend at least 4-6 weeks making a focused effort on improving your position, you'll notice that eventually you won't need to think about it as much and you'll naturally fall into a more confident appearance.

ASSERTIVENESS TRAINING

Eyes

Maintaining good eye contact is one of the critical elements of non-verbal assertiveness communication. It's all about finding the right balance though; if you look away too often, you'll look nervous and unconfident. On the other hand, if you always maintain a stony stare, people may think that you are a bit creepy. So it's best to maintain firm eye contact, but to pepper in a few breaks every once in a while to make the other person feel just right. If you find that the person you are talking to is giving you an icy stare, you can stand your ground by giving back a soft gaze between their eyes.

I had a tough time maintaining eye contact at first. It was one of those things that I found most challenging. However, it is practically impossible to be seen as confident if you tend to be looking at everything but the eyes of those you're talking to, so I placed a massive emphasis on sorting this out.

ASSERTIVENESS TRAINING

Your main goal with eye contact is simple: you should make your partner feel comfortable with you. A simple trick is to try and match your eye contact with that of your partner's. This advice often works because people feel comfortable with different levels of eye contact. To calibrate this, notice the amount of eye contact that they feel comfortable giving you, and then try to match it. Look at your partner in the eyes when they are looking at you, and look away when they aren't.

However, you don't want to mirror your partner exactly, or you'll come across as a mime as they notice that you are copying their every move. The best way to avoid this is to wait a few seconds before matching them. Wait a few seconds before either looking away or at them.

ASSERTIVENESS TRAINING

Voice

Just as most things in assertive communication, it's all about finding the right balance; shouting is just as bad as talking in a whisper. They both project a lack of confidence. Whenever you shout, you instantly lose credibility, as it makes you seem as though you're trying too hard to make others hear and pay attention to you. On the other hand, whispering projects that you lack confidence. The sweet spot would be right in the middle, using a well-modulated voice that not only commands respect but makes others see you as self-assured. Try to prevent your voice from wobbling or trembling and speak at a volume that is loud enough for everyone to hear you without having to resort to shouting.

-Slowing down is important. Whenever you take deep breaths and slow down the speed of your voice, your voice tone will usually come out better.

Whenever you feel nervous, your voice tends to be a dead giveaway of your current emotional state, as it will go up a few notes, and you'll start to talk quicker than usual. These are clear signs that you are afraid or anxious. Slowing down helps you altogether avoid this. The words that come out of your mouth will easier to understand by the slow pace and your tone will probably lower.

Hands

Your hands are invaluable "tools" that you can use to emphasize the points you make during a conversation. Whenever you use affirmative hand gestures, you will add an air of confidence to your message. If you need to emphasize a point, you can try bringing your hands up and putting your fingers together (a gesture known as steepling), because in many cultures it is seen as the universal sign of confidence. You should avoid fidgeting with your hands, and doing quick or jerky movements with them, as this will signal anxiety and significantly detract from your words.

ASSERTIVENESS TRAINING

To smile or not to smile

It's surprising how much of an impact smiling has on how others perceive you. You can be easily mistaken for a sad, uninteresting, or negative person if you avoid smiling. On the other hand, if you know how to smile correctly, people will tend to see you as friendly and positive and will want to be around you more.

When dealing with a situation when you're nervous or feel uncomfortable, it's easy not to be aware of the look that you have in your face, which usually means that you'll have a sad or unconfident look that others will be quick to notice.

To avoid this, work on your smile. Smiles can be tricky because they can quickly come across as fake or creepy. How do you know if you're smiling correctly? It's quite simple actually: check if your whole face is involved in the smile.

ASSERTIVENESS TRAINING

Smiling is not only about moving the lips, but it's about moving the cheeks upward and making the eyes crinkle a bit, causing them to narrow and sometimes even appear closed.

Although it's not necessary to show your teeth when smiling (I had a challenging time with this because of my severely crooked teeth, which I didn't get fixed until my late 20's!), it can be a nice plus. If you're not comfortable with showing your teeth, rest assured that it's not necessary.

Smiles can be used in critical moments to your advantage: for example, when meeting or greeting someone, when you want to express joy, when you call people by their name, and when you say goodbye. You can also use smiles to help keep debates or disagreements in a friendly tone. Smiling helps let the other person know that you aren't merely attacking them, even if you don't agree with what they're saying

CHAPTER 3: THE ASSERTIVENESS BOOT CAMP

Developing assertive beliefs

Our mind-set and beliefs have an enormous impact on our actions; what we say and how we feel is deeply influenced by our state of mind. It's typical for issues to crop up whenever we have a different set of beliefs about ourselves and others.

If you can adopt the right beliefs, then it will be much easier to become more assertive, as it is only natural for the behaviors to follow the mind-set. On the other hand, without the right beliefs, then you will always struggle to maintain an assertive communication style.

ASSERTIVENESS TRAINING

The essential assertive principles are:

-Everyone has the exact same set of rights.

-I have freedom over what I think and the decisions I make.

-It's human to make mistakes, learn from them, and improve.

-No one but myself is responsible for my actions and responses.

-I don't need permission from others to take action.

-I have the right to disagree with others. It's not possible to agree

ASSERTIVENESS TRAINING

On the other hand, some beliefs hinder us from acting assertively, by making us think we are not equal to others by either influencing us to respond passively or aggressively:

-I do not provide the same value as others. Others are better/more intelligent than me.

-I am more intelligent, valuable, or authoritative than other people.

-My opinion doesn't matter much.

-The world is harsh, and it's essential to get others before they get me.

-If I do not succeed at everything I do, I'm a total failure.

-Asking is a weakness; one must tell people what to do.

-I'd rather keep quiet and say nothing than to speak up my mind.

How to develop the right mindset

If you're reading this book, you probably have more non-assertive beliefs than assertive ones. The good news is that it's possible to replace the old beliefs that are hindering you.

-To start, you must pay attention to how your current mindset and beliefs drive how you act in the world.

-Notice which of your beliefs you'd like to replace, then identify the ones you'd like to replace them.

ASSERTIVENESS TRAINING

To help you remember your new beliefs, write them down in places where you're able to see them. Write them down on pieces of paper and place these in your room, office, or even car. You could also get creative and put these in places like your phone or computer's wallpaper.

-Every time after each social interaction you have through the day, make sure that you check your list of assertive beliefs and see if you were able to apply them or not.

-Make sure that you capitalize on your successes. Pay attention to how adopting new beliefs helped you.

ASSERTIVENESS TRAINING

How being too nice always might not be a good thing

There is no doubt that our society would benefit from more acts of kindness because we live in times where egocentric behaviors are cheered on and imitated. Nice people are no doubt great at bringing some goodness into this world, but sometimes kindness can be taken to the end of the spectrum, where it starts becoming harmful to the person acting this way.

Let's take a look at some of the things that commonly happens when you tend to be too nice to others, too often. It's important to mention that: there is no doubt that kindness should be encouraged and appreciated, but never when it comes at the expense of your happiness or wellbeing.

ASSERTIVENESS TRAINING

People will take advantage of your kindness

When you start prioritizing other's needs above your own, others will quickly take note and will start expecting that you treat them like royalty at all times. I remember, on several occasions, how difficult it was for me to say no to others. I secretly hoped that once I made their request, they would like me more or treat me better, but this was seldom the case. They started asking me for more and more favors and expected me to say yes every single time.

It's perfectly fine to say no to requests if you're feeling overwhelmed or don't agree with others. If you start to believe that your opinion or well-being aren't necessary, people will have no problem walking all over you. Remember that only you are responsible for looking at your own needs first because there's no one else that will take care of that for you, not even your loved ones.

ASSERTIVENESS TRAINING

People will only seek you when they need something

One of the toughest parts about being overly nice is that a lot of people will start treating you as a means to an end. These people will seek you often whenever they require something. Remember that people aren't able to take advantage of you unless you let them. If you can set firm boundaries, others will quickly know when they've gone too far. And you can still help those who deserve it without putting your needs last.

You will be constantly let down

Since you are always trying to please everyone you meet, you will start expecting others to do the same for you. Unfortunately, the vast majority of people won't be as kind as you are to them, which will ultimately leave you frustrated and disappointed.

ASSERTIVENESS TRAINING

You will attract the wrong kind of people

A lot of people tend to act overly nice as a way to seek attention from others. If this is your case, remember that you will attract the wrong kind of people into your life – especially people that are needy and demanding. Sometimes, being overly nice is a way of being selfish, because you start to look outside to fill a void that you haven't been able to fill yourself. Since you have minimal self-worth, others have a hard time recognizing your value too.

Because assertiveness is such a powerful antidote to negative emotions such as fear, shyness, and anger, there are a lot of situations where this communication style is appropriate. For instance:

-Whenever you want to speak up, make a request or ask for favors while at the same time making your rights be respected.

It also helps keep the fear that prevents you from doing these things at bay.

-To express complaints or disagreements without hurting other people's feelings.

-To respond to intimidation or criticism without further inciting aggressive behavior.

-To express positive emotions and give compliments the right way.

-To carry a conversation from beginning to end calmly and comfortably.

-To be able to share your feelings, thoughts, and opinions with others while still having their respect.

-To handle minor annoyances before you take a defensive or aggressive stance or make an aggressive response.

So how do yo u start?

The first step for passive people wanting to become more assertive typically starts when they've recognized that they're being taken advantage of a lot or find it extremely difficult to say "no" to requests that they don't want and they've had enough. Others may have realized that they're losing a lot of friends and the respect of their colleagues or co-workers because they aren't able to keep their aggressive behaviors in check. Others might not see themselves as unassertive, but they do feel a bit unfulfilled in life as they do not know how to express their needs and emotions the right way.

ASSERTIVENESS TRAINING

You and pretty much everybody else can cite an instance when they've acted aggressively, or they've been able to communicate their thoughts. Some people use these as proof to deny that they're not unassertive. The reality is that most of us may have an easier time being assertive in certain situations (when interacting with our family for instance) but may have a difficult time saying "no" at work or we may have a hard time accepting compliments or disagreeing with others.

It's essential to avoid falling into the victim mindset and realize that it is crucial to correct the situation yourself. No one else will do this for you.

The first steps

There are several ways to compose assertive responses. Ideally, an assertive response should contain several parts:

ASSERTIVENESS TRAINING

-Describe the person or persons you're communicating with the troublesome situation through your eyes. It's essential to be specific about time and actions, and it's best to avoid making accusations, such as "you're always unsupportive," "you're always upset in the mornings," "you never notice my efforts." It's best to avoid accusatory words such as "you" or "you're." They suggest that the person you're communicating with is a jerk.

-If possible use "I" statements, as they make you take responsibility for your opinions and emotions. If possible, try to emphasize positive feelings connected to your goals instead of any possible resentment you might feel for the other person. For instance: "I feel like my efforts aren't being noticed because I haven't had a promotion for two years even after all of my successful projects."

ASSERTIVENESS TRAINING

-You should also be clear about any changes that you'd like to see, but always make sure that the requests are reasonable, by being considerate of the other person's needs. Also, you should keep an open mind and be open to making some changes yourself in return. If there should be any effects or consequences if the other person does or does not make the desired changes, describe them clearly. These consequences shouldn't sound as dire threats.

-Once you've done this, it's time to practice giving assertive responses. With the responses you have developed, try asking a friend or family member to help you out, or use a mirror to role-play the interaction. You can start with simple real-life situations and work up to more challenging ones as you get more comfortable.

As you practice, especially if you're doing so with a training partner that is playing his or her role realistically, you'll notice that merely rehearsing the assertive responses won't be enough.

ASSERTIVENESS TRAINING

Sometimes, it will seem that no matter how calm or courteous you try to be, your response will sound like a personal assault to the other person. The person you're interacting with should act out the more natural responses. In a lot of cases, it won't take much to handle the situation: merely explaining your behavior and standing your ground should be enough. Sometimes, you'll need to use other strategies mentioned in this guide.

-Once you feel comfortable practicing assertive communication in a wide variety of situations (especially those that you find the most challenging) with your training partner or with the mirror, it's time to move to the real life. It's essential to take it slow and start with more relaxed situations that don't cause you a lot of stress. It's best to build up some confidence and make slight adjustments as needed instead of trying to go the full way and not get the results you expected right away.

-Try to find ways to improve your assertiveness in your everyday life. For instance, ask for directions, return a defective item, or ask a friend to lend you something. If you're participating in classes, try asking the instructor to go over a point you didn't quite understand again.

If you have a hard time saying no to people, start by saying no to people you already feel comfortable with and then move to more challenging situations such as dealing with a boss or employer. Call up government officials or police officers whenever you have a complaint about something or if something is bothering you. If possible, try to keep a written journal of your progress so that you can be aware of your progress as you go along.

Learning to say no

For most people, especially those that mostly use a passive communication style, it can be challenging to say "no" to requests.

ASSERTIVENESS TRAINING

Why are those two letters so hard to say? In most cases, it boils down to fear of rejection. People that are afraid to say "no" to requests are fearful that they will disappoint others, hurt their feelings or appear rude or aggressive.

When you were a child, you were probably very good at saying no to most requests, and you did so without any guilt or shame afterward. So why did it become so difficult to say "no" as you grew up? Usually, it's because you learned that it was rude to say no to your authority figures, such as your parents and teachers. Saying "no" was offensive and saying "yes" was the polite word to say. As we grew up we likely held on to our childhood beliefs and associated "no" with being selfish or poorly mannered.

The first step towards learning how to say no is to understand that your time and needs are valuable. Going through life always seeking the approval of others is a recipe for constant unhappiness.

ASSERTIVENESS TRAINING

If you currently have low self-esteem and are struggling with this, remember the following:

-The problems of others do not define you.

-Your needs and time are valuable and unique. There's no one else in this world that can offer the same things as you can.

-It's human to make mistakes; everyone has done things they've regretted.

Before you say yes to someone, it's essential to decide if it's worth it or not to accept the request. It's very likely that on several occasions you've been in the position where you've committed to something and had lots of second thoughts and doubts afterward. As a result, you then start to think of ways to get out of the situation.

You may even have to resort to lies to get out of the situation. Think about all the negative emotions you felt whenever you said yes to someone just to please. You probably felt resentment, anger, and stress because of it.

How to say no with confidence:

-Do not hesitate. It's better to be clear and direct and say "No, I can't" or "No, I don't want to." Doing this is much better than to be apologetic and give all sorts of reasons.

-Be honest. What a lot of people tend to do is to use a made-up excuse after saying that they cannot do something. But remember that this will inevitably lead to feelings of guilt, which is the very thing we're trying to avoid.

-Think about the stress and anguish that saying "yes" has brought you before in similar situations.

-Don't even say "I'll think about it" if you already know you don't want to do it. The only thing that will result from this is prolonged stress.

-Keep in mind that your value is separate from what you do for others.

-You can add a polite remark at the end, but make sure it doesn't sound sarcastic. Something simple like "No, I can't, but thanks for asking" is enough.

Once you begin to say "No" often, you'll notice that feelings of resentment or guilt will start to melt away, and you'll begin to feel empowered and more confident, which is just what we're looking for!

Assertiveness in specific situations

Assertive communication tends to work well in most situations, but there are some cases where using it is not quite simple. The three most common conditions where it might be tricky to behave assertively are:

-When dealing with unrealistic demands.

-When dealing with criticism

-When receiving compliments.

These situations tend to catch a lot of people off guard because they are dealing with a situation where their own wishes and the wishes of others are not aligned. As you know by now, this is precisely the time where being assertive is most helpful.

So let's learn how to navigate these tricky scenarios.

How to deal with unrealistic demands

Dealing with unrealistic demands can be a tough experience, and it's not always easy to remain assertive in those circumstances. Never forget your assertive rights: everyone has the right to say no to a request.

The next time you are facing a demand, consider if there are factors such as stereotypes that may be influencing your actions. For example, let's say that you're a manager at a big company. Most people expect you to work a lot, and to have little time for yourself. These kinds of generalizations tend to harm by placing ridiculous demands that are associated with specific roles in society.

ASSERTIVENESS TRAINING

When rejecting unreasonable demands, it's essential to:

-Make it clear that you are rejecting the request and not the person. Things can quickly sour if you are not communicating clearly.

-Once you decline or say no, it's essential that you stick to your guns and not give in to pressure. If others notice that you eventually crumble under pressure, they will quickly see this as a weakness and exploit it. Of course, in some cases it can be a good idea to change your mind, so don't be afraid to do so if circumstances change and you're respecting your needs and time.

-Some people, especially those that deal with passive people that rarely say "no" to their requests and demands on a day to day basis, feel that they are entitled to the time and attention of others. It's vital to set clear boundaries with these people as early as possible.

-Remember that you have the right to say no without having to apologize or justify yourself

Receiving criticism

-There are not always good intentions behind criticism. Whenever you're dealing with criticism, take a moment to see if you can notice if it's honest criticism or if there are other reasons behind it. Often, people that are angry or frustrated tend to throw negative criticism to whoever is standing in front of them.

-The best way to respond to criticism is by saying it back. For instance, say that someone thinks that you dress sloppily. You may answer, "So you feel that I dress sloppily." You should acknowledge any valid elements of the criticism, even if they sounded harsh.

-A typical response to avoid when being criticized is giving back criticism. Doing this doesn't provide anything of value and tends to promote aggression.

-If the criticism is genuine, make sure that you ask the person giving it for any suggestions and also thank them for pointing it out.

-If you need to give feedback to others, it's essential to make sure that you are criticizing the action and not the person. To soften the blow, you might even begin with an appreciative comment such as "I know that you've worked very hard on this project, but…". Avoid using accusatory words and sentences.

How to handle compliments

For a lot of people, handling compliments can be troublesome, as they don't know which response to give.

ASSERTIVENESS TRAINING

It's not uncommon to end up in awkward situations.

Remember that compliments are a positive way of giving support to others. People tend to give compliments so that they can help increase the other person's self-esteem and confidence. If the praise is not met with an appropriate response, then the person giving the compliment is less likely to give another one in the future.

The best way to handle a compliment is to thank the person that complimented you and accept it, regardless if you do or do not agree with it. Some simple phrases that you can use are "Thanks! That's very kind of you to say" or "Thank you, I enjoyed doing X thing, but it's great to hear that you liked it."

On the other hand, if you're the one giving a compliment, make sure that the praise is genuine, as others can easily detect insincerity and this can hinder a person's sense of self-worth instead of helping it. Remember that it is beneficial to give others positive feedback, as it tends to be remembered more easily than criticism.

CHAPTER 4: ASSERTIVENESS IN THE WORKPLACE

Why employers tend to prefer assertive employees

Modern workplaces are much different than what they were not too many years ago. Work culture is evolving at a swift pace, and so is the attitude of both employers and employees. The most successful professionals today are bright, corporate savvy, and aren't afraid of standing up to their beliefs, even when they don't agree with what their boss is saying. Of course, there are exceptions, but today's best employees have realized the importance of letting their bosses know what they're thinking; they know that it's not necessary to say 'yes' to every single thing that others request.

ASSERTIVENESS TRAINING

Because of this, many wonder whether employers and managers prefer assertive employees or not. Interestingly, today's employers are on the lookout for signs of assertiveness during the recruiting or interview process.

Let's take a look at why assertiveness is such a desirable trait:

Assertive people tend to be great at solving problems. At work, this translates to the employee being able to address multiple office and customer-related issues with ease. People who tend to be too passive in their approach have a harder time handling these workplace issues. On the other end, employees that lean more towards the aggressive side tend to cause unnecessary conflict that is never desirable.

ASSERTIVENESS TRAINING

A big part of working in an organization is the ability to work with others and being able to communicate well with co-workers and superiors. Assertive employees can do this in a constructive manner. They are also are more effective at expressing their thoughts without hurting others. Smart employers and recruiters know that assertive people tend to be more productive, since they have a lot of confidence to back up their independent decisions, without necessarily having to wait for their boss or manager always to give them the green light. They also know when it's essential to ask for some clarification to perform their assigned tasks to the standard expected from them.

An assertive employee is also able to stay calm and process criticism without resorting to anger or resentment, both of which can cause issues in the workplace and affect productivity and results.

ASSERTIVENESS TRAINING

Assertive workers have an easy time interacting with co-workers and know when the right time to delegate assignments is. They also make for good team meeting leaders as they are great mediators.

Nowadays, one of the most critical parts of a business is customer service. Many of the most successful companies in the world have got to where they are primarily thanks to their reputable customer service. Assertive workers can communicate and connect better with customers and listen to their issues or complaints while asking the right questions so that they can help resolve their problems. Whenever it is not possible to solve the customer's problem, they know how to politely apologize and tell the customer they are unable to do more, without hurting their feelings or compromising on the company's principles.

Some companies have even chosen to implement assertiveness training sessions, as they know about the potential they have to benefit their employees.

ASSERTIVENESS TRAINING

It is no secret that workplace tension is often the result of sub-par communication and uncontrolled emotions, both of which are quickly addressed with assertiveness training.

Companies that have implemented assertiveness training effectively have noticed that destructive and hurtful tensions between their employees reduce significantly. Something interesting tends to happen: assertiveness promotes more assertiveness. Assertive employees, because they are more confident about themselves, have an easier time recognizing and accepting the strength of their co-workers and superiors, which helps boost their productivity. It is rare for an employee not want to cooperate with an assertive co-worker. For a manager, this is a win-win situation. The overall workplace atmosphere becomes that of healthy competition within the team. Everyone is pushing others to perform their best positively.

ASSERTIVENESS TRAINING

Another essential reason why employers prefer assertive employees is that assertive employees have an easier time accepting their failures and mistakes. Because of this, they will be much more proactive at trying out new ways of doing things in order to improve their productivity and will be eager to participate more in the workings of the company; they also won't keep quiet when they're asked to suggest ideas and won't shy away from taking the initiative. This proactivity not only helps the employees acquire more responsibilities and climb the corporate ladder but also keeps inactivity at bay.

When people at work are always worried about not stepping on other's toes or upsetting their bosses or employers, they avoid expending a lot of negative energy. A positive side effect of this is reduced stress levels in the workplace, which is related to again, an improvement in productivity. Since people aren't as worried about what others will think about them and aren't scared of making mistakes, they can better focus on the most critical aspects of their jobs.

There are other less obvious benefits too, some of which affect employers or managers. In most companies, it is common to give performance appraisal to the employees. In these appraisals, it's sometimes necessary to give feedback that can cause a lot of tension between the employer and employee. It's not always easy to give negative feedback, and it can be even more challenging to be able to conduct these meetings with uncooperative individuals. Because assertive people can keep a cool head when receiving criticism, managers have an easier time maintaining a good level of positivity when conducting performance appraisal evaluations.

There's no doubt that assertive employees are seen as being more honest, with higher levels of integrity by others, when compared to those who aren't. Of course, not every employer or manager will value assertiveness. Some of the less savvy ones will feel threatened by assertive individuals, as it is one of the most well-known traits of effective leaders.

However, the smarter employers will encourage their employees to be more confident and vocal, because they are aware how effective leadership is not about controlling others, but about helping others instead, leading by example and supporting positive behaviors. In the end, it should all be about creating a company culture where everyone's opinion has some weight.

How to act during a job interview

There are several myths surrounding face to face job interviews. One of the biggest ones is believing that the person that conducts the interview has all the power and control, and because of this, the interviewee should take a more passive approach, allowing the interviewer to decide the course and tone of the interview. To a lot of people, this makes a lot of sense, but as mentioned, this is simply a myth and one that often ends up harming the interviewee's results and performance during the interview.

Interviewers who use this approach are not aware that this way of doing things results in rarely finding the best option for the position.

No matter how much you want to land the job, it's essential to realize that employers also have their needs, and those needs often tend to have a high degree of urgency; they need to find the best person for the job with the best possible candidate, as quick as possible.

There are several reasons why interviewers fail to meet that need, and they only emphasize the need for you to act more assertively to help tip the balance to your favor.

Interview processes are rarely optimized for efficiency. Most people seeking jobs often assume that they are, but in reality, most companies rarely stay current on the optimal practices for hiring.

ASSERTIVENESS TRAINING

They might emphasize experience over competency, which is a recipe to overlook potentially great candidates that have less experience but better long-term potential. They could also have several preconceived notions that will work against you even before you open your mouth.

Keep in mind that it's important to remain assertive during the face-to-face interview and never cross the line towards aggressiveness. You already know the difference between the two. You will probably stand out using any of the two approaches, but by being aggressive, you'll surely make the wrong kind of impression.

When seeking out for a job, remember not to buy into the interview myth. Instead, choose to act more assertively and approach the interview as a give and take conversation between equals. The results will probably surprise you.

ASSERTIVENESS TRAINING

Being assertive with your boss

Imagine that the clock in your laptop reads 6 pm, and you unconsciously start to feel nervous as you are aware that there is still a lot of work to be done, but it's officially time to leave the office. You are afraid of how your boss might react to you leaving while there's unfinished work. Will he/she get angry at you if you decide to go home and continue tomorrow? Is it worth it to take a stand with your boss?

When you are part of an organization, you inevitably have to deal with different kinds of situations daily. You will be interacting with co-workers and bosses that you will often hesitate to confront when something is bothering you. In many cases, you will need to be able to say what's on your mind and that's where assertiveness becomes very important.

ASSERTIVENESS TRAINING

Most people feel naturally intimidated by those that are in positions of authority, and it's often an inevitable result of our upbringing. Most children are taught to respect their teachers, parents, and guardians. A lot of bosses and managers aren't afraid to use intimidation tactics to have better control of their employees, adding fuel to the fire. It is no secret that intimidation and fear of authority are widespread in a lot of organizations. As you practice being assertive, you'll quickly notice that it's harder to apply certain principles at the office than they are at home or with your friends.

But intimidation and fear of authority don't have to be part of your reality. Being assertive at work shouldn't be a stress-inducing experience. On the contrary: it should be an essential stepping stone for you to improve your overall quality of life. A healthy organization is one where all employees are empowered to express their thoughts and opinions to their bosses and managers.

ASSERTIVENESS TRAINING

Let's take a look at some advice that will help you become more assertive when dealing with superiors at work:

Assessing if it's worth it

Before you confront a boss, you have to keep your energy in check. Your mental, physical and emotional energy are all affected whenever you are addressing someone about an issue. If you are only wasting your energy unnecessarily, you'll probably decrease the chances of achieving the goals you want.

While doing this assessment, you have to keep the bigger picture in mind and question the organization as a whole, so that you can examine if it would be better to use your energy somewhere else or not. If you find out or are aware that your boss has been demoralized by the organization, he or she will likely be replaced soon by someone else.

It's a massive waste of time to confront someone in this position.

Avoiding mistakes

When you act assertively, you are standing up for your beliefs while respecting the opinion of others. If you think that a superior is about to commit a big mistake and it will damage the organization, it's probably a good idea to intervene.

However, before you do so, it's essential to make sure that you're right. Double-check your facts and be prepared to answer your superior's questions. If you realize that the problem lies with your boss, you have to be willing to accept the effects of your confrontation.

Only pick the right "fights" and go to great lengths to understand the root cause of the issue.

When you feel ready to speak to your boss, ask to do so in a private manner so that you can present your findings and thoughts calmly. If you choose to do so in front of others, while there is a lot of tension or chaos going on, the result will rarely be positive. Calling out someone's mistakes in front of others can have disastrous effects. On the other hand, approaching your superior in a calm and collected manner will encourage him or her to respond the same way. If instead, you remain courteous and honorable without being too passive, you'll be more likely to achieve the results you seek.

Dealing with difficult superiors

You'll often have to deal with superiors that aren't kind or supportive towards you. Difficult bosses or managers include those that try to belittle you, intimidate you, or try to take advantage of you. Passive employees will suffer out of fear of losing their jobs. Aggressive people will lash back without giving too much thought to the consequences of their actions.

ASSERTIVENESS TRAINING

Instead, you should always judge the situation appropriately. Even good bosses or managers might snap under pressure and do something that they will quickly regret. If you're dealing with such a case, it's often better to ignore the situation. But if you're instead dealing with a bully that seems to love being in the position of power, it's better to step in and act instead of allowing them to take advantage of you.

Discrimination is also another unfortunate common problem in many organizations. It's also another case where being assertive will be your best bet. A lot of superiors will have a natural preference for certain employees, but discrimination has no place in any organization. If you notice that your superior is favoring someone and offering them the best assignments or projects just because they like them and not because of their professional performance, it's time to speak up.

The same advice applies it's essential to confront them privately and calmly so that you can explain to them the situation. You should make it clear that you will not accept their unprofessional behavior. If the abuse or discrimination continues, make sure to document the unacceptable behavior in as much detail as you can so that you can contact the HR department later.

Negotiating with your boss

Employees tend to have a hard time discussing their salaries or vacations with their bosses. They are afraid of risking their position by coming across as demanding, lazy, or greedy. However, employees who do their job responsibly can sometimes ask for better pay, more responsibilities or more vacation days. Of course, you should always be smart about it, and always consider the overall situation you are in before moving forward.

For instance, if you know that you've had a very consistent performance lately and you've had the same salary for a while, it's fair to ask for a raise.

When negotiating with your boss, it's essential to remain respectfully assertive. Expect your boss not to agree always. When this happens, ask him the reason why. If he's not willing to give you vacation days or a raise soon, he can at least tell you where you can improve or what you need to do to get what you want.

Dealing with being overworked

It's common for employees to want to work a lot to please their superiors, often motivated by wanting better assignments, a raise or a promotion. In some occasions, it is fear that drives them.

ASSERTIVENESS TRAINING

It's ok to go through specific periods where you're working more than usual, but it's essential to know when to stop. As this can soon become a habit and you'll inevitably feel burned out. You've also got to remember that bosses are often dealing with several situations at once, and they might not be paying attention to your health whenever they assign you new tasks. In the end, they want things to be done.

If you feel like you've done way too much at work, it's best to admit to them that you're feeling overworked and that your health and performance are starting to suffer. In some cases, your superiors will try to press you, but it's essential to stand your ground and say "no" to their requests.

We also live in an era when it's easy for employers to contact their employees whenever they want, thanks to the advances in communication technology.

ASSERTIVENESS TRAINING

Superiors often give out several tasks at once, and they are often looking to delegate so that they can get everything done. Because of this, a lot of employees end up working a lot of hours after they've left the office. Working on weekends at home has also become the norm, which can be very disruptive to anyone's private life. Because of this, it's wise to limit your interaction with your boss outside of work hours. If they continue to push on, be assertive by merely saying that you're not available and maintain your position.

Standing up for yourself when dealing with authority figures isn't easy, but it's essential if you want to have better control of your life. Being able to speak to your boss and ask for what you want, or offer an alternate plan of action that you think would work better means that you're well on your way to become a more assertive person.

ASSERTIVENESS TRAINING

How to be assertive in everyday work-related situations

Can you think of a co-worker or colleague that can come out of challenging situations unscathed and with a great deal of professionalism, no matter how tense the circumstances might be or how difficult the personalities involved are. Try to think of someone that has a fantastic ability to deflect negative emotions such as anger and frustration, while choosing not to settle for an outcome that would affect his self-respect or compromise his values. That would be someone that is very adept at being assertive in business or academia. For those that tend to be passive, avoid confrontation like the plague or aren't temperamental, their qualities may seem almost supernatural to others.

To cultivate this attribute in the workplace, let's take a look at some examples of the most common situations you might find yourself in, and the best ways to approach them:

ASSERTIVENESS TRAINING

When you need to get others to back you up or behind your plan.

Imagine that you're working in a team that is working on a new project and you've just got an excellent idea. You have weekly meetings with your co-workers, and you've decided to propose your plan of action in the next one.

A passive employee would wait for the leader to make the first suggestion, and then agree to what he has to say. He or she would probably keep quiet instead of suggesting ways to improve the project.

On the other hand, an aggressive employee would present their idea as being the best choice, and if in the leadership position, begin to assign tasks to others. Whenever someone tries to suggest alternatives, he won't pause to consider them.

The best approach, the assertive approach, would consist of listening to the various suggestions of your co-workers and making sure that their strongest points are acknowledged. Imagine that someone suggests a few exciting ideas for a marketing campaign. They also suggest to make the campaign longer than you think would be wise. In this case, you could tell them that you liked the ideas, but that it's best to shorten the marketing campaign so that you can test if they will work out in the real world or not. By doing this, you have successfully contributed to the conversation and have made others feel valued and appreciated. The consequence of this will be that those whose ideas you've acknowledged will feel more motivated to back you up when you need others to support your suggestions.

When you're in charge of an underperforming team

You've been recently assigned to lead one of the most challenging groups in the company.

ASSERTIVENESS TRAINING

A team that is known for having several individuals that roll in late to work every day always argue and are very inefficient.

The passive leader would fume about the poor performance of his subordinates and even take up some of the slack without doing anything to fix the issues going around.

The aggressive leader will confront the problematic subordinates and ask them why they are always late at work and constantly arguing with their co-workers. He will also tell them that their behavior makes them un-hireable anywhere else and that he's doing him a big favor by keeping them in the company and not firing him. Of course, this only makes the problematic employees angry and resentful and prevents them from improving their or behavior in the workplace.

The assertive leader will choose to have a private meeting with each of the problematic employees. He will then let them know why their behaviors are not acceptable while being careful not to hurt their feelings by aiming at their personal qualities. He will also ask them if there's any particular reason why they're always late at work. By being emotionally intelligent about the situation, they are more likely to open up and cooperate. They might be having some issues in their personal lives that are hurting their performance and affecting their behavior and focus at work. Or maybe they are having a hard time understanding the instructions of their leaders. The assertive leader realizes the importance of improving his relationship with his subordinates, so he organizes a weekly meeting to check-in and enhances communication.

As you can see, no one loses by taking the assertive approach. By taking control of a situation in an emotionally intelligent way instead of letting the issues continue to linger on, both sides win.

When you'd like a promotion, but things have stayed the same for a long time

Imagine that it's September and in January you spoke to your bass and asked that you'd like a promotion. Back then, your boss mentioned that he was not able to give you the promotion because the company was not able to give any raises due to financial issues. However, he said that if your performance is excellent, he will do whatever he can to promote you and raise your salary.

A passive employee would carry on feeling disappointed and frustrated without ever speaking with his boss about the matter again. He or she would then complain all the time with his co-workers about the situation because they feel that their efforts have not been acknowledged.

ASSERTIVENESS TRAINING

An aggressive employee will confront his boss and tell him that he has been looking for new opportunities elsewhere because he feels that he has not been appreciated and treated correctly.

The best approach would be to ask to speak with your boss again and mention how you've been doing a great job all these months so that you can finally get the promotion. Your boss may then tell you that it's still difficult for the company to give you a raise. At this time, it's best not to let feelings of anger of resentment cloud your mind and instead ask for more information on the organization's future. Ask if there are any tangible goals that you can shoot at that can be reviewed the next time you ask for the promotion. Using this approach, you're showing several desirable attributes such as resilience, maturity, collectedness, all coupled with a desire to improve.

When your morals are compromised

Sometimes, your morals and work end up clashing against each other. Imagine that you were firmly against animal cruelty, and you get assigned to a project that involves the promotion of a makeup product that was tested extensively with animals. Let's take a look at how the passive, the aggressive, and the assertive employees would react.

The passive employee would feel frustrated that he was assigned to the new project. He wonders if he should say something to his manager for a while, but decides not to. After all, he recently leased a car. He becomes involved in his project and ends up feeling a lot of resentment and anger towards his employer and himself, even though his employer is not aware that he has firm beliefs that clash with animal experimentation and cruelty.

ASSERTIVENESS TRAINING

The aggressive employee has also leased a car, but he decides that he won't be participating in the project, as it goes against his morals, and he's firmly opposed to unnecessary animal cruelty. He storms inside his manager's office and tells him in a rude tone that he doesn't want to be involved in the project at all and that if he's forced, he will quit. His manager agrees not to force him to participate in the project. However, he takes note of his inappropriate behavior and ends up not giving him the raise he was planning to because of excellent performance.

The assertive employee has also leased a car recently but decides to talk to his employer, as he's firmly opposed to participating in a project that involves testing on animals. He realizes that his employer probably has no idea that he is opposed to animal cruelty, and brings up the subject calmly. He explains how he'd feel like he's compromising his values by participating in the project but also values his job.

His employer appreciates the fact that he has been honest with his opinions and understands his point of view, so he decides to assign him to another project that has no connection to animal testing at all.

When you lack the skills to perform an assignment

It's normal to want to accept work that is beyond your current abilities. Especially employees that are looking for a promotion or a salary raise, they will want to take on tasks that are challenging, hoping that their boss or manager takes notice and rewards them accordingly. Others will want to explore new possibilities and expand their current skill set and will take on extra work because of this. It's never a bad idea to step outside your comfort zone and push yourself. After all, that's how you can improve in a short period.

However, picture this scenario: your team leader has assigned you a task that is entirely out of your reach. You're working in the I.T. department, and they've asked you to help with some graphic design stuff. It could take you days of research, stress, and frustration to be able to perform the task to the expected level.

The passive employee would agree to take the task while keeping quiet about how it's ultimately beyond their abilities. After several days, they realize that they have made little progress and deliver subpar results in the end. They then complain to their co-workers and speak badly of the team leader.

The aggressive employee would tell the team leader that they don't want to perform the task because their expertise is in I.T., and they don't want anything to do with graphic design.

The assertive employee would choose to talk with the team leader and explain the reasons why they don't think that they would be able to deliver excellent results. They emphasize how they don't want to put the company's project on the line unnecessarily. The team leader thanks them for being so honest and then looks for someone else that's better suited for the task.

When your safety is compromised

Imagine that you are working in construction and that your employer has asked you to do an important task, but you lack the necessary equipment to do so safely.

The passive employee would carry on with the task, fully aware that his safety will be compromised. He doesn't feel comfortable to tell his employer that he lacks the necessary equipment to do the job without risks. He nervously performs the task and fortunately isn't injured.

ASSERTIVENESS TRAINING

However, if this trend continues, it's just a matter of time until an accident occurs.

The aggressive employee shouts to his employer, telling him that he won't do anything until he's given proper safety gear and tools.

The assertive employee decides to evaluate the situation more carefully. He realizes that his wellbeing might be compromised and decides to talk to his employer calmly and explain to him the job. He mentions how such dangerous situation, regardless of the pay, isn't worth taking chances without having the proper gear. He says how he doesn't want to jeopardize his well-being, and his employer decides to put the task on hold until his company has enough money to invest in the proper safety gear required.

Assertiveness in business meetings and presentations

If you've been working in an organization for a while, the following scenario probably feels familiar to you: you are participating in one of your company's meetings, when you suddenly have a great idea that you're confident will benefit the current project or assignment you and your team are working on. After deciding whether to speak up or not, you tell others about it but choose to downplay it significantly because you are afraid of putting others off, especially your teammates. Because of this, your idea then doesn't sound as exciting as it did when it first popped into your mind.

Business meetings are yet another situation where being assertive pays off big time. However, it's essential to act intelligently. It's not necessary to appear overconfident. Do not accept other's ideas unless you feel convinced about them.

If you say yes to your boss or team leader without being sure how to perform a particular task, you are probably digging your own grave in the workplace.

Here' some simple advice that goes a long way whenever you find yourself participating in a business meeting:

Be well prepared.

Before the meeting even starts, you can accomplish a lot by being well-prepared. As you probably know, most meetings rarely stay on course, but it's still a great idea to sit down and think about what you'd like to achieve in it.

The mistake many make though is that they only focus on this and, at the time of the meeting, keep their mouths shut out of fear of disapproval or shyness.

You should not only think about your ideas and the points you'd like to get across but also how you would like to come across yourself. Try to spend some time focusing on "who you want to be in the meeting." We all have an inner voice inside our heads that will either help or hinder us. Be aware of any negative thoughts, and try to do your best to leave them at the door. If you are having a difficult time shutting up any negative voices inside your head, you might benefit by doing short meditation sessions to have better control of your thoughts. If you have a clear picture of both what you'd like to say and how you'd like others to see you during the meeting, you'll feel prepared for anything.

Sticking to your ideas and morals

A lot of people get into the bad habit of lying or compromising their morals to please their superiors. Never forget that a business meeting is only a formal discussion with your co-workers and superiors.

Some might feel the pressure and share fake numbers to look good in front of others, but this will probably backfire at some point. Also, it is complicated to have assertive body language while you are worried that others might find out the truth. Your body can quickly reflect what you're genuinely thinking, and you probably won't come across as confident or assertive.

Speak the right way

There is an easy "hack" for those that lack some confidence when speaking in front of other people: try to talk like a newscaster. If you've ever heard a newscaster, you've noticed that they are direct but never abrupt. They also speak with buckets of confidence, and you never hear them say "um" or apologetic words. Imagine that you're almost reading lines from bullet points. Just try not to sound too robotic. Your body language should support what you're trying to say and how you'd like to come across.

ASSERTIVENESS TRAINING

If your shoulders are hunched over and you are often staring at the floor, avoiding eye contact, your ideas, as good as they might be, won't pack the same punch. All the body language advice mentioned previously applies here. Try to sit or stand up straight and don't forget about looking others in the eye, especially managers or bosses that need to fully grasp what you're saying.

What to do about interruptions

In almost all meetings there will be interruptions. There is virtually no way to avoid them. Picture this: you are explaining how to implement your new plan to your managers, and then someone starts talking, completely cutting you off and almost ignoring you. Whenever this happens, just let the person finish what they're saying instead of trying to interrupt them yourself, as it might turn into a "who can interrupt the other the most" contest.

If you keep getting interrupted, don't be afraid to tell them in a non-offensive manner that it's essential to let you finish what you were saying before they can talk.

Don't be afraid to get external support

All of the above advice is great when applied, but sometimes it won't be nearly enough. There's no point in ignoring your shortcomings. Some people, even those that know how to be assertive in certain situations, have problems with public speaking or talking in front of a group. If something or someone is making you anxious, there is no shame in discussing the situation with your co-workers and teammates so that they can step in and help you if necessary. If you're not the best in presentations, seek advice from someone else, maybe a superior that you think is quite skilled at talking in front of others. All that is left afterward is to practice until you feel more confident; at first, you might start by giving presentations to your family and friends until you feel more at ease to do it at work.

ASSERTIVENESS TRAINING

Being an assertive leader

How would you feel if your team was led by someone overly passive? You'd probably won't feel as motivated to reach your goals and get out of your comfort zone often. Leaders that are too aggressive are a whole different story, as they do sometimes motivate people, but negatively. If there were one skill that the majority of leaders would benefit from improving, it would be assertiveness.

Being assertive is extremely useful in most areas of your life, but it can be especially powerful appropriately used by a leader, as it can magnify a lot of essential leadership qualities. There is more damage done by not being assertive enough as a leader than by being too assertive. Leaders that can balance this crucial skill with their other leadership qualities will be able to motivate others to work their best and reach the goals that have been set.

Let's take a look at some of the benefits that being assertive will offer to those in leadership positions:

Promoting an environment that welcomes new ideas

Some of the most successful companies in the world are filled with managers and leaders that can challenge and push back on their superiors. They don't do this to be rebels, but because they stood firm whenever they wanted to ask for new resources or disagree with ideas they think would have severe effects for the company. Being in this environment means that plans have to be considered profoundly to justify a course of action.

Improving your connection with others

Assertive leaders can focus on healthy relationships that can significantly benefit their organization.

These same leaders are also great at making clients notice problems that they hadn't thought before, due to their ability to challenge and push them back. In the end, this creates a great impression on the clients, as well as more perceived value.

Promoting teamwork

An assertive leader helps teams thrive by making every team member feel appreciated by letting them express their thoughts and ideas. A confident leader knows how to create a safe environment where even less popular opinions can be heard, increasing everyone's chance to participate fully.

ASSERTIVENESS TRAINING

What to do if you're a passive leader

Of course, most leaders certainly struggle with being assertive, due to many reasons: they might have lots of self-doubts or be driven by the fear of not being liked by the majority. You might already be leading a group of people at work, and by reading this book, you've realized that you are a passive leader. If you're unsure, check if you exhibit some of these qualities:

-You hesitate a lot when you're speaking with others.

-You try to avoid conflict, even if it will cost you or your organization money and resources.

-You are quick to blame yourself whenever something goes not as planned, even when it's not you or your team member's fault.

-You make bold claims out of fear, without facts to back them up.

-You rely a lot on the opinion of others instead of yourself whenever you make a decision.

It's essential to use the correct management style, as it will definitively have a significant impact on the tone for your entire team. If you want to get excellent results, being assertive will help it make clear that you're the leader.

By being an assertive leader, you will help keep others focused on your company's primary goal, whatever it might be, and help your team members remain productive and deliver results. You have clear expectations, but at the same time, you listen to others and are flexible.

ASSERTIVENESS TRAINING

Aggressive leaders only care about winning, even if it means stepping over the feelings or needs of others. They only take what they need, often without asking. An aggressive leader usually works with a team that can deliver results, but his subordinates tend to act out of fear and intimidation rather than because they'd like to work with someone to reach the best result. The reason why we see more aggressive leaders than assertive or passive ones is that it tends to be very easy to abuse a position of power.

Then, there are some leaders and managers that tend to employ a "tantrum" method of leadership, which has a lot of drawbacks when compared to the benefits, as it causes their teams to be very fearful of their outbursts, which chokes most innovation and creativity.

Whether your current leadership style is passive or aggressive, there are several things you can do to start moving towards being more assertive.

ASSERTIVENESS TRAINING

Let others know what you believe

Making sure that your whole team understands your leadership philosophy can be incredibly useful. If necessary, write it down and make sure that your entire team understands it. You have to explain what you believe and expect from your team members, and what they can expect from you. Make sure not to say things that you won't be able to back up or live up to afterward.

Maintain consistent expectations

If you have consistent expectations of your subordinates and staff members, acting assertively will be the best choice. For instance, if you expect to have a specific project ready in a time frame that you've been very clear about, then it's only natural if you assert your authority whenever it's not delivered on time since it's rooted in a well-understood expectation.

Don't make the mistake of thinking that others can read your thoughts; whenever you speak, try to do so clearly, so that everyone understands your message clearly.

Clear instructions are one of the "secret weapons" that many effective leaders use. Being direct and clear should also apply when you are giving criticism to others. Avoid doing false flattery as it provides no benefit to your team and organization. Give praise to those that have rightfully earned it.

Standing your ground

An assertive leader is expert at avoiding manipulation and scare tactics, whether it is by other team members that want to offload work unto them unfairly or when dealing with aggressive superiors that are trying to intimidate them. Don't be afraid to say no to requests that sound unreasonable.

At the same time, try to keep your emotions in check; as you know, having controlled emotions is a big part of effective leadership development, so that you don't become angry or frustrated.

Do not hesitate when making decisions

Leaders with little self-confidence or those that are too passive tend to have a hard time taking decisive action. This delay not only prevents progress but can also create new issues. While you should never act before thinking, you should do your best to gather all the facts you can about a situation and trust your knowledge and instincts to make decisions.

Handling failure

Effective leaders know that failure is a normal part of the road to success.

Make sure that both you and your team are capable of embracing failure. Be very clear about this with your team, and let them know that while you expect them to reach the goals. There are things that you can always learn from a loss. A team that is afraid to fail is one that is afraid to try out new things. Whenever this happens, it won't be long before the majority of the suggestions and plans to come from the leader, and no leader can have all the good ideas and answers.

Controlling your emotions

Aggressive leaders tend to lash out to their subordinates regularly whenever things don't go according to their plans. It's natural to feel angry or frustrated from time to time, but you should avoid these emotions from influencing your actions and thoughts. Whenever you feel like someone, or something has pushed your angry button, take a few breaths, meditate, or do whatever is required for you to calm yourself before taking action or communicating with others.

ASSERTIVENESS TRAINING

Remaining professional and cool-headed in even the most stressful situations will earn you the respect of your teammates and staff members because they will be aware that you even when you are displeased you do not display rude or unprofessional behavior.

CHAPTER 5: ASSERTIVENESS FOR WOMEN

Even though there has been a lot of progress done over the last few decades, the voices of women are still less loud and influential than those of their male counterparts, especially in certain areas, such as the workplace and politics. It's still common to see women that rarely speak up for themselves and avoid conflicts in general. And unfortunately, whenever they choose to speak up, their voices are not acknowledged as they should be, and in many cases even ignored.

In this chapter, we will take a look at some strategies that can help women develop an assertive style of communication that will help them express their ideas and wants assertively, as they tend to have their own set of specific challenges.

There is no way around the fact that if women want to be successful as possible at work or become influential in particular environments, they need to be able to develop an effective way to communicate their ideas and opinions.

How female communication differs

Research has found that women tend to use a softer, cooperative form of communication that tends to be highly effective at avoiding conflicts. This can set women back in a lot of environments where a communication style that is either competitive, aggressive, or assertive tends to stand out. Unfortunately, certain prevailing gender stereotypes are still being used to justify why women don't tend to speak up and be assertive. For instance, the unfair perception that women's value is based on their looks rather than their accomplishments and knowledge. Or the impression that they should be stay-at-home mothers whose primary role should be to attend to the needs of others.

Even though none of the above are fair, for most, these views are hardly compatible with assertiveness.

Women have to work with a smaller range of acceptable behaviors, especially in specific environments such as the workplace. If they are perceived as being too nice, they could either be seen as too weak or even manipulative in some cases. On the other end, when they act aggressively, people are quick to think they're acting "unladylike." To make things more unbalanced, whenever men show traits that are often associated with women, such as nurturing, empathy and generosity, they are applauded for being progressive. Whenever men are commanding, competitive or aggressive, society tends to be ok with them, since they can justify it with "men act more aggressive and competitive by nature, due to their higher testosterone levels."

ASSERTIVENESS TRAINING

Research has shown that males tend to interrupt more than females, do more bold interruptions in public settings, and speak more than females in situations where status is essential. This fact is ironic, given the prevalence of the stereotype, "women speak too much." Also, in private environments and situations, such as the family home and a when living with a partner, women and men don't have an equal say in both small and significant matters; women tend to be at a disadvantage because of the relations of power that remain.

So, it seems to be in most environments, men tend to not only speak up more but generally speak more than women. We should also ask ourselves if it's the number of words or a speech's impact that denotes real power. After all, it's more important that our words have a real effect rather than just trying to speak the most phrases. And even then, men's voices tend to have more of an impact because, in our current society, they often tend to occupy more roles of power or status.

We shouldn't blame men for this inequity, but on our society as a whole for holding onto damaging stereotypes that prevent progress. Men will have a more considerable impact on society as long as this inequity remains because whenever women speak up and act assertively or competitively, a lot of people aren't ok with it. For real change to happen, collective mobilizations need to take place, and harmful paradigms need to disappear.

In the meantime, however, there is a lot that women can do to find their way to speak up more and be more assertive.

Women and assertiveness in the workplace

The workplace is of especial importance to both men and women, and it is here where women tend to be their own worst enemies. It is not uncommon for women to be afraid to advocate for themselves.

ASSERTIVENESS TRAINING

People often believe that the workplace is a meritocracy and that all that's needed is their willingness and ability to give good results what matters to make progress. However, this is a deeply flawed belief. The workplace is many things but rarely is it a meritocracy. Of course, good results tend to be rewarded, but not always. The people who tend to get ahead of others are those that are willing to speak up, advocate for themselves, and face conflict head-on.

Women that want to succeed in the workplace should know who they are, the value of their knowledge, their experience, and their worth to their company or clients. It's ok to do a little self-promotion, after all, most people that become successful in the workplace do. Men tend to be especially good at this.

It's essential, however, not to mix up confidence with arrogance. There are ways to promote yourself and your accomplishments without coming across as obnoxious.

Promoting yourself is especially important in meetings with superiors that often aren't fully aware of their employees' achievements, ideas, results, and contributions. It's simple: if others don't know about your results and accomplishments, then you will not get as many opportunities in the workplace (and in other areas of life as well).

Here are some of the biggest things that set back women from achieving the results they want in the workplace:

Avoiding conflict.

Often, women tend to excel at making connections and building relationships. Networking and relationship-building can be extremely useful in the workplace, and in some environments this is an unavoidable part of becoming successful.

Both men and women tend to avoid conflict, but women can be more reluctant to disagree with their co-workers. This fear stems from being afraid to alienate people. The fear of being seen as a 'bitch' can fuel women to be as friendly and easy-going with everyone as possible. However, conflict doesn't necessarily have to be upsetting or disagreeing, as long as you can leave emotions out of the situation. Most assertiveness advice in this book works well for this.

Always keep in mind that work relationships often need to be strong, but should never be mixed up for personal friendships. Your primary objective at work isn't to make friends, but to get the job done and work well with people. It's essential to find the right balance between being someone that helps create a harmonious workplace and being someone that can speak up and be acknowledged.

ASSERTIVENESS TRAINING

Fearing assertive speech

One of the most common and fatal mistakes that women make in the workplace is softening their speech. As you already know, we can be either passive, aggressive, or assertive in all three components of speech: non-verbal communication, choice of words and voice tone. Women tend to avoid being assertive in all three of these.

Women tend to use what is known as "soft language." Examples of these are the following non-assertive phrases: "This is probably the best option," "This could be the solution to the problem," or "We might all want to consider doing x thing." Instead, a more assertive way of saying those phrases would be: "This is the best option," "This is the solution to the problem" or "I would like to try doing x thing."

It's best to say what you mean and avoid trying to soften or qualify it.

Of course, it's essential to be aware of who you're interacting with and then decide the approach you'd like to take with them. For instance, if you are dealing with assertive or aggressive people, then it's probably best to stick with an assertive approach. But if you're instead dealing with people that tend to act very passively, it's best to back off a little. There's also a time and place to soften your body language, choice of words and tone of voice, but if you go too far, people will have a hard time seeing you as a leader. Proper calibration is the key here.

Avoiding negotiation

The inequality of men vs. women at work continues with salaries. Men are still ahead of women in this area.

On average, women earn around 20% less than their male counterparts, and this applies not only for those working in organizations but for those that work independently too. Research has found that a large part of this discrepancy is due to women's tendency to avoid negotiation. Females tend to feel guiltier when asking for more money, so they often end up saying yes to the first offer.

Women that prefer to avoid negotiating should realize that they are worth to their company or their clients and charge accordingly. You must always remember that no one else will do it for you, especially if you are self-employed.

Most women might even be aware of the fact that they are being too nice and still avoid using assertive behavior, as mentioned previously, often out of the fear of being labeled a 'bitch.'

ASSERTIVENESS TRAINING

This fear can sometimes be so intense that it affects women's behavior in several different ways: how they speak to others, the type of body language they use and the type of treatment they accept from others.

Tiny actions tend to have a significant impact on communication. For instance, certain subtle word choices tend to weaken the strength of women's voices in the workplace. Sometimes, making small adjustments, such as altering the way how you say things, can go a long way to help reclaim some lost territory. Remember that it will be very tough to advance in your career if you don't assert yourself correctly. Being assertive in the workplace is not only a positive thing, but it's a real necessity nowadays.

Let's take a look at some practical advice that usually has quick results when applied correctly:

Avoid apologizing too much

Don't get me wrong. There's definitively a time and place where apologies are essential preserve a relationship. But they are not necessary in most cases, and can even be detrimental to the image you want to project to others. For instance, if you tend to say "I'm sorry" every time someone asks you to move aside so that they can get to the coffee maker, it's highly likely that you are overly apologetic in several circumstances of your life.

Ironically, those two words also can make urgent demands sound like requests. Let's compare the following two options.

-"I'm sorry, but I think that the team would be productive if we all made sure we arrived early."

-"The team would definitively be more productive if we all arrived early."

As you can see, the first sentence sounds as though we are giving the team an option, so don't be surprised if people take it that way and forget about the "request" soon after.

The second sentence sounds much more like a powerful statement, and one that asks for a response. It seems as though we are saying orders without sounding too bossy.

Stop making your statements sound gentle

Besides saying, "I'm sorry," there are several other commonly used phrases that tend to sabotage women by taking their message and weakening it.

For instance, "Could you please do me a favor" and "I was wondering if" are a couple more. Phrases like these tend to creep up often, and each time they are used, they weaken your voice. Try to say what you mean and what you want without apologizing if it's not necessary. Watering down your words will only affect you negatively. It's best to say what you mean to be better respected and understood by others.

Quieting the negative inner voice

We all have an inner voice that seems to be nagging us constantly, telling us that what we want to say has no value to others or that we are uninteresting. Instead of feeding this inner voice, try to channel your energy into listening and learning, as you'll be better able to follow a conversation and have an easier time thinking about good ideas to contribute.

ASSERTIVENESS TRAINING

Having reasonable expectations

Although much of the above advice helps peel away layers of 'niceness,' it's essential to have reasonable expectations not only of others but of yourself too. Remember that nobody is perfect and that some situations will be more complicated than others. If you are in a team leadership position and a new employee makes a mistake, use the situation to help them learn from their actions so that they can improve next time. If you find yourself making an embarrassing comment at a meeting, make sure that you are better prepared in the next one so that you can make better suggestions.

There will also be people that feel intimidated by strength in women. There will also be those that don't want to be held accountable for their actions and will be on the constant lookout for flaws in others so that they can attack their ideas or personalities. Avoid giving in by mirroring their negative behaviors.

By being assertive and not backing down, you'll present yourself in a way that others will hear, understand, and hopefully align with your thinking.

Assertive body language for women

Have you ever met someone that seems to have a great background, knowledge, and skills but yet, they seem to have a tough time advancing in their career or finding suitable job opportunities? You might have a lot going on for you: a great degree, solid performance reviews, strong recommendations, etc, but if you have very poor body language, you probably won't get the promotions and opportunities you rightfully deserve.

While most assertive body language advice we've covered tends to be equally useful for both women and men, there are a few "hacks" that will be especially helpful for women:

Don't be afraid of taking up more space

Timid women are very conscious of the space they are taking. They usually keep their arms close by their side and even tuck their feet under their seat in order not to take up too much space. If you want to show some confidence, it's crucial to claim some space; you can easily do this by firmly planting your feet about a shoulder-width apart when standing up. If you are sitting, don't be afraid to lean back a bit in your seat and use the armrests.

Steepling

If you press the tips of your fingers together while your palms facing towards each other in front of your torso, you'll be doing the universal sign of confidence, known as steepling. This sign can be especially useful when done at a meeting or when talking to others to emphasize a point. For some reason, it is especially effective when done by women.

Building rapport

Building rapport is essential for both men and women, as it is how you can network and get along with your co-workers. There are a few things that you can do with your body language to help build rapport with others. The first is pointing your feet. We subconsciously pay attention to people's feet, as it tells us the direction they wish to go. Have you noticed when you're talking to someone, and they have their feet pointed towards the door? It always makes you feel as though they are itching to leave. To keep others engaged with what you have to say, you might want to point your feet and angle your whole body towards the person you're speaking. Subtly mirroring their posture and movements also goes a long way to help you bond with someone.

CHAPTER 6: ASSERTIVENESS IN RELATIONSHIPS

When couples start spending a lot of time together, such as when they get married and live in the same place, they usually believe that they are on equal footing, and that their marriage or decision to live together backs them up whenever they want to express their feelings and needs with the expectation that they will be respected.

In reality, there is absolutely no guarantee that it will in all cases. Sooner or later, most people in partnerships start to feel uncomfortable due to imbalances in their relationships. These imbalances can be caused by many reasons, but probably the most common one happens when one partner asks the other to do something they don't want to do.

It could be doing activities they don't enjoy, hanging out with people they dislike or deciding how they want to spend their money. In these cases, whenever a partner doesn't agree with a request but isn't able to say "no," they quickly start adding negative baggage to the relationship.

There could be other reasons why imbalances in relationships may occur, though. For example, when someone is too dominating when discussing things and rarely allows their partner to have a voice, or if they do, they don't give enough importance to what they have to say. More passive partners tend to allow this behavior to go for a while, as they would prefer to avoid conflict if possible.

The previously mentioned imbalances tend to be more common when a partner is overly aggressive partner and the other an excessively submissive one.

ASSERTIVENESS TRAINING

This imbalance creates a state of play in which the aggressive partner exerts a lot of control over the other, keeping them from having equal rights and say in their relationship. Even if the couples are not arguing with each other or accusing each other from inappropriate behavior, there is a strong imbalance going on, where one partner passively accepts situations that he or she doesn't like, while the other takes control of their relationship.

To clarify, we are not talking about an abusive relationship, where the more passive partner is fearful of their partner due to emotional, physical or sexual mistreatment, but a partnership that has a strong pattern of communication imbalances.

ASSERTIVENESS TRAINING

Becoming more assertive in a relationship

If you are currently in a relationship, and you've realized that there is a communication imbalance going on, it's not difficult to recognize whether you are the passive or the aggressive partner. Even if you are the aggressive partner, you will benefit from replacing the aggression for assertiveness, as it will definitively help your relationship in the long run.

It can be tough to measure the level of equality in a partnership. Even if you are consciously attempting to make sure that both of you have an equal say in all matters, it will probably never be perfectly balanced. What is more realistic though, is to aim for a relationship where both members know that they can stand up for their rights and express their beliefs and feelings without feeling afraid of the consequences; a healthy relationship where both are confident in their requests, as they try to make them as reasonable as possible, while refusing unreasonable ones.

ASSERTIVENESS TRAINING

What we are talking about is a relationship where both partners feel entirely free to assert themselves.

In most relationships, this is not the case, as there is a lot of passive, aggressive, or ego-centered behavior going on. Submissive partners tend to be overly agreeable with the requests of their more aggressive partner, and often collect a lot of negative feelings that eventually affect the relationship. Their style of communication leads them to avoid situations where there might be conflict, as they get very uncomfortable just at the mere thought of it. Because of this, they don't get the opportunity to voice their opinions and end up continually doing things they don't enjoy.

On the other hand, aggressive partners openly express their wants and get their needs met, but achieve this in a way that often damages their relationship, as they forget about the needs of others while they do so.

The last-mentioned relationship style is ego-driven. Ego driven partners are not always necessarily aggressive and can be even assertive at times, but their motivations are ego-centered. People that have ego-centered behavior place little importance on their partner's needs, because their main desire is to be the center of attention at all times. They want to make sure that their wants are always met and their opinions heard and acknowledged no matter what. They might do so assertively sometimes, but they usually resort to aggressiveness if it's required to get what they want. They tend to be so focused on this that they pay little attention to their partner's needs.

After a while, in most relationships, a clear pattern of communication emerges. Of course, nothing is set in stone: sometimes a partner might favor a particular style depending on what would work best for them at a time. But usually, a dominating pattern can be seen.

However, if both partners decide to relate and communicate with each other assertively, the relationship is off to a where a harmonious balance is more likely.

Factors that influence the development of relationship styles

There are several factors that have influenced your style of relationship, and the two main ones are your childhood upbringing and your self-esteem. When you were a child, you observed your parents behaviors and noticed how they communicated with each other and shared their thoughts and emotions. You subconsciously stored these observations. As you grew up, depending on your personality type, you either embraced these behaviors or you rejected them. Because of this, you relate to friends, family members and loved ones in a way that is either similar or very different to what you experienced in your upbringing. These same behaviors are the ones you then bring to your relationship.

If one of your parents tended to have an aggressive style of communication, then you probably accepted that as the standard norm, which made you behave similarly. On the other hand, if the parent you related to the most was submissive, then you might feel that acting this way is the natural way to respond to your partner.

Your self-esteem also plays a significant role in how you relate to those close to you. If you have poor self-esteem then that might manifest itself in your relationship by being overly passive and non-assertive. It is likely that your low self-esteem makes you do as much as you can to keep your partner happy, even at the cost of your happiness. On the other hand, if you have an over-inflated ego coupled with unhealthy self-esteem, then you will probably have an ego-centered communication style with your partner, where you mostly care about your own needs and not those of your partner, and you have an arrogant expectation of what you want at the expense of others.

ASSERTIVENESS TRAINING

If you or your partner have developed a non-assertive style of communication, it can be easy to get stuck in a pattern of ineffective communication that can end up harming or even ending the relationship.

No matter what current style of communication tends to dominate your relationship, it is possible to develop a more assertive style and begin communicating more effectively with your partner while not forgetting about his or her wants and feelings at the same time. For the best results, it's crucial that both you and your partner replace the passive, aggressive, and ego-centered behaviors with assertive ones. It won't work if only one partner puts in the effort and decides to make a change alone.

Let's now take a look at some of the most effective strategies to have a more assertive relationship

ASSERTIVENESS TRAINING

Always consider your intentions

Pretty much everyone has been guilty of initiating a conversation or raising a touchy subject without giving it too much thought. Can you remember a few conversations where you've started talking without having the slightest idea of what you want to accomplish or where you'd like to get at? A worse situation is where you decide to bring up a separate issue when your partner is talking about a separate one. As you already know, this rarely, if ever, accomplishes anything.

Whenever you raise an issue or start a discussion, try to have a purpose in mind, as the outcome will almost always be better this way. Don't forget what you'd like to express to the other and keep in mind your intentions, especially if things start to become complicated or heated.

Accept that it's not always possible to win

We all would like to be right. The sense of pleasure that being right gives us can be a powerful motivator. Because of this, a lot of people in relationships become fixed in being right and are guaranteed to lose in the long-term because of this.

The term "lose the battle to win the war" fits perfectly here; sometimes, you have to consider if it's better to let go of your need to be right for the bigger picture; which could be things such as having a more stable relationship, and being more supportive of your partner's needs. If you keep a long term goal such as these in mind, the small battles won't seem like such a big deal.

Attentive listening

Whenever you have a general conversation or discussion with your partner, it is essential to use careful listening skills. For each of you to listen attentively to each other, both should be paying attention to not only the words spoken, but to the body language, facial expressions and even the emotions behind the messages said. You should emphasize trying to be authentic when getting your message across so that your body language and everything else works in harmony and doesn't send mixed signals that might confuse your partner. It's even a good idea for both partners to pause after talking for a while and summarize what the other has said to see if the other is clearly understanding what they're saying or not.

In relationships, it's not enough to treat the other as an equal that is not better than yourself. You should also fill your communication with empathy and compassion to cause a real positive impact on your relationship.

When both partners do this, they will have an easier time genuinely understanding each other, and things will naturally improve.

Avoid forcing your partner to change

One of the most common issues arises when a partner has the objective of making the other change. The problem with this is that whenever you start discussing a topic, you have already set up a structure where the listener will have to defend himself. Positive changes come over time and rarely by force.

If you find yourself trying to regularly change the ideas and behaviors of your partner, then what you are communicating to them is that what they already have to offer isn't good enough. This can quickly push them away and create some distance between you two.

Making solid plans and having clear agreements

Most couples tend to forget these two, as evident as they might sound. A crucial part of having an assertive style of communication in a relationship is that both agree on the outcomes they would like. Doing this is an essential step because it binds all the other strategies and gives a solid resolution to your relationship communication. If you forget to do this, you'll leave each conversation without knowing precisely what was achieved. Make every agreement clear and straightforward to understand, so that there is no distortion and doubts between the two of you.

Implementing assertive communication in your relationship

Most of the standard assertiveness guidelines apply when you and your partner are trying to improve their relationship communication style.

Again, using assertive "I language" is an excellent way of communicating your thoughts and feelings to others and taking action to make sure that your needs are being acknowledged while respecting your partner's rights at the same time. It also helps you use clear and direct messages in order not to distort your assertive message.

Using "I language" is much better than using accusatory language and pointing fingers. It helps you seem as though you are fully responsible for what you are saying. It also helps create a non-threatening atmosphere that promotes cooperation and not intimidation.

By continuing to use "I language," you will both reinforce what you want and stand firm on what you don't want.

For instance, let's look at an example where someone is interested in fishing and would like to take his partner on a fishing trip.

ASSERTIVENESS TRAINING

However, his partner isn't too keen on this activity.

If "I language" is correctly implemented, then the dialogue between them might look something like the following exchange:

Partner A) "It's been a while since I haven't gone fishing and I would love it if you went on a fishing trip with me. I think that this would be a cool activity to do together".

Partner B) "I appreciate that you want to include me on your fishing trip, and I like how you were looking for activities to do together, but I do not enjoy fishing. Maybe we could set aside some time to talk about activities that we both might enjoy".

As you can see, both partner A and partner B used "I Language" to express what they wanted.

ASSERTIVENESS TRAINING

Even though partner a didn't get the response he was looking for, partner B's assertive communication style now allows for more effective communication, and might help find a simple agreement as to which activity they can do together.

Now, let's imagine that Partner A is not happy at all with the result and starts to insist more and more. At that point, he'd be crossing the line by wanting their partner to accept his request while not listening to their wants. Even if this happens, the conversation can continue being free of conflict if enough listening and "I language" is used. The continuation of the dialogue might look like this:

Partner A: "I really would love it if you went together with me on the fishing trip. We don't get a chance to do a lot of activities together, and I think that this is something you would enjoy if you tried it. I have always loved fishing, and I'm confident that you'd enjoy going on this trip with me".

Partner B: "I thank you for considering me for the fishing trip. However, I dislike being on a boat and the idea of waiting long hours to catch fish doesn't appeal to me. Please, let's think of other activities we might do together."

By continuing to use "I language," the conversation might continue to be civil. However, in some cases, it will inevitably steer towards an aggressive communication style, especially if one partner is not listening fully to the wants of his or her partner and becomes more persistent in his demands. Even if this happens, you can continue to use assertive "I-Language" to bring some balance back to the conversation. If your partner continues to pressure you to change your way of thinking, then be firm in your resolve while remembering to be respectful.

Following the above example, let's see how the conversation might continue if Partner A continues to be persistent.

ASSERTIVENESS TRAINING

Partner A) "We are never able to do things together because you always have some excuse and you never consider me."

Partner B) "I'm sorry that you feel like that, but I don't want to go fishing."

Partner A) "I can't believe you don't want to go with me. This is something I'd love to do with you, but you don't want to cooperate".

Partner B) "I'm sorry that you feel that way, but I don't want to go fishing. I would love to try other activities with you, though".

As you can see, Partner A is starting to feel frustrated that Partner B isn't accepting his invitation to go fishing, and it shows in his choice of words.

ASSERTIVENESS TRAINING

However, Partner B is trying to bring some balance by maintaining an assertive communication style. The conversation could continue for some time until they find a solution, but it is crucial to keep using an assertive communication style even if your partner steers off course.

Implementing an assertive style of communication in your relationship is undoubtedly useful for improving your mutual understanding, but it might take a while for couples to fully incorporate it into their lives, especially if they are heavily used to aggressive, passive or ego-driven styles of communication. Because of this, it's crucial to support each other whenever you want to implement any long-lasting positive change in your relationship. With collaborative support, partners can help themselves when doing a transition such as this.

For instance, you might notice that your partner is used to a passive style of communication and has a tough time asserting his or her needs.

ASSERTIVENESS TRAINING

If you see this, you can help them draw attention to their behavior and improve how they implement assertive language when talking. On the other hand, if a partner is too aggressive or dominant, it might be a good idea to remind them when they are steering off course.

As with any other area of your life, implementing assertiveness inside your relationship won't come naturally at first, and it won't be realistically possible to use it all the time. But if you practice daily to bring assertive behavior into your relationship, you will quickly find improvements in your partnership thanks to the mutual respect and understanding that this communication style brings to the table.

CHAPTER 7: Dealing with Hostility and Manipulation

In nature, it is not uncommon for animals to display a flight or fight response whenever there is conflict. In modern civilization, however, it is no longer acceptable to fight with others openly anymore. It is more common to take on the abuse or to grit our teeth and make empty vows of revenge. Fleeing away from the situation or the conflicting person tends not to be an option to many of us. Our fight or flight instinct makes feelings of fear, anger and frustration crop up, which then may lead to mood disorders such as depression and anxiety.

It's practically impossible to go through life without dealing with aggressive and confrontational people at some point.

ASSERTIVENESS TRAINING

We may encounter these individuals pretty much anywhere: in our social circles, at work, and not surprisingly, even in our homes. Some people tend to resort to tactics such as counter manipulations, but such responses rarely work well and don't tend to get us the results we want.

Hostile individuals might be adept at coming across as overbearing or demanding, but with the right approach and the use of assertive communication, it is possible to disable such unwanted behaviors and sometimes, even turn aggression into cooperation and confrontation into respect.

There can be endless reasons why people choose to resort to confrontational or hostile behavior. Some of the most common are pathological anger, mental trauma, substance abuse, excess stress, sociopathy or psychopathy, etc. Most often it boils down to only having a bad day.

Whatever the reason, you must know how to respond the right way, especially when your rights and safety are being threatened.

Let's take a look at some of the most effective ways to handle hostile or confrontational people.

Prioritizing your safety

Not all confrontational or hostile people are worth your time. Especially since most of the times, your happiness and even your well-being might be negatively affected. So keep in mind that unless there's something important to you at stake, it's best to avoid interacting with people that are acting overly hostile.

Also, your number one priority when dealing with confrontational people if they become too aggressive should be to protect yourself.

If you don't feel safe or comfortable when in such a situation, it is best to leave. There is no shame in looking for outside help (such as law enforcement) when needed.

Remain calm at all times

Aggressive individuals tend to be skilled at projecting their aggression onto others and pushing people's buttons to keep them off balance so that they can have the upper hand. If you let them, they will easily exploit your weaknesses. Whenever you need to deal with difficult people, the number one strategy will always be to keep your cool. The less reactive you are to an aggressive individual's provocations, the better you'll be able to use good judgment handle the situation appropriately.

Whenever we feel upset or angry, we can often say things that we might quickly regret.

If you start feeling as though you're reaching your boiling point, start taking deep breaths and count slowly to 5 or ten. By the time you've made a few breaths, you'll notice that you're no longer as angry as before and will be better able to figure out a better response to the situation you're dealing with, instead of acting irrationally and exacerbating the problem. If you find that you are still feeling very angry or frustrated after taking several deep breaths, it might be a better idea to take a time out and revisit the issue later, if you have that option. You might even tell the other person, "I would rather talk later" or "let's deal with this after we both calm down."

Put yourself in the other person's shoes.

It can be challenging to honestly try to put yourself into a hostile person's shoes, especially when someone is working hard to push your buttons, but if you can do so even for a brief moment, you will be able to handle the situation better.

To help you with this, you can ask yourself what could have caused the hostile or aggressive person you're dealing with to act that way. For instance "My co-worker is acting very aggressive and demanding today. It must be difficult to be in his position and have to pick up the slack of a lot of lazy people in our team".

Of course, there is no real excuse for aggressive behavior, but it's useful to remind yourself that most aggression tends to be driven by some suffering.

Avoid acting passively

A lot of aggressive people tend to be skilled at picking on those that they see as weaker. Because of this, if you always remain passive and compliant, you'll be an easy target for bullies. Bullies tend to be very insecure and weak on the inside. This fact is true for bullies found everywhere: from schools to the workplace, and even our homes.

ASSERTIVENESS TRAINING

Whenever you need to deal with a bully, make sure that you do so in a position where you can be safe. If necessary, have other people around as support. If the abuse or aggression starts becoming physical, verbal, or emotional, it's best to consult with law enforcement or legal professionals on the matter. It's always important to stand up to bullies, and it's not necessary to do so alone.

Whenever you're dealing with hostile people, you should always keep in mind everyone's assertive rights so that you can recognize when someone violates yours or when you are starting to cross the line and affect other people's rights. If you can keep calm and not cross the line and harm others, then you have all the right to stand up for yourself.

As mentioned, it's essential to avoid interacting with a hostile or aggressive person, unless there's something at stake. Whenever there's no other way out, it's best to deal with the situation by remaining assertive.

ASSERTIVENESS TRAINING

How to handle manipulation

Manipulation is a disguised form of aggression. Whenever someone attempts to control your behavior so that they can meet their wants by using guilt, anxiety, ignorance, fear, or power to their favor. Manipulators can be found everywhere in your life, from your home to your workplace.

A very common strategy done by manipulators is to set up arbitrary rules that suit and benefit them. They might invent regulations and standards of what is right and wrong and their standards of reason and logic. People tend to become manipulative simply because it's a strategy that worked for them in the past, so they decide to continue being this way as a means to get what they want.

There are several ways to deal with manipulators while remaining assertive.

Let's explore some of the most useful strategies:

Fogging

Fogging is a strategy where instead of arguing back, you give a minimal and calm response while using terms that aren't hostile or defensive, but at the same time, you don't agree with the manipulator's demands. The name "fogging" comes from acting as a wall of fog into which hostile responses are thrown but never returned.

Example:

-A) "I've been waiting for you for almost 30 minutes. I'm growing tired with you letting me down so often."

-B) "Yes, I'm aware that I've arrived later than expected, and I can see how this has affected you."

-A) "Of course it has affected me. I've been waiting for almost half an hour. Don't you care about other's time at all?

-B) "Yes, I was worried that you would be left waiting for me for that long."

-A) "Then why were you late?"

As you can see, person A started with an aggressive statement, but person B started using "fogging" since the beginning. Because of this, Person A's manipulative or aggressive tactics had little to latch onto, and he won't be able to continue for long. Whenever you offer agreement instead of disagreement to someone using aggressive or manipulative tactics on you, they typically expect an aggressive response thrown back at them, since it's most people's natural way of responding. But how fogging works is by taking aggressive people by surprise and giving them an unexpected response.

It's an effective way of "sidestepping" their issue while letting you retain your viewpoint and integrity since you are agreeing with what they're saying.

Let's take a look at another fogging example:

-A) "You behaved pretty stupidly in that party. What was going on in your head?

-B) "Yes, I can see why you think I behaved stupidly."

The broken record technique

Another useful technique is "Broken Record." Here you remain calmly persistent and repeat your request again and again, with a relaxed tone of voice, without showing any signs of anger or annoyance.

ASSERTIVENESS TRAINING

Example:

Imagine that someone just bought an electronic device, but it quickly died, and they want to return it to the store. Let's see how to apply the "Broken Record" technique in this situation.

-A) "I bought this tablet a couple of days ago, and the battery is not working properly. Instead of lasting around 8 hours, it dies off after around 5 hours of use. I want a refund, please.

-B) "The battery duration on this model depends largely on which kind of apps you are running. It may sometimes last as little as you are reporting".

-A) I've only been using standard, non-demanding software, and it still dies off after around 5 hours of use. I want a refund, please.

-B) "You cannot expect me to give you a refund just because you say that the battery lasts slightly less than 8 hours".

-A) "The battery lasts less than what I expected, and because of this I would like a refund please"

And so on.

The main idea of the "Broken record" technique is to keep repeating the same request so that the discussion doesn't become side-tracked. It also helps avoid talking about irrelevant things that might make you or the person you're talking with angry or defensive. The main idea here is to remain calm and be direct and transparent with your request. Stick to what you'd like to achieve and be persistent.

In some cases, you won't be able to get what you request. If you feel that your self-respect is not being affected, and the other person offers you an alternative, you can accept the compromise. Of course, only take a settlement if you are okay with the agreement and it doesn't affect your self-worth.

The negative inquiry

Whenever you're interacting with others, you'll inevitably have to deal with criticism at some point or another. While not all criticism is bad, some will definitively be unfair and undeserved. The technique of "negative inquiry" can be advantageous when dealing with criticism.

This technique helps you learn more about critical comments (whether they were just or undeserved) and is often a much better response than reacting defensively or aggressively.

ASSERTIVENESS TRAINING

Let's take a look at an example of this technique:

Two co-workers are having lunch together. And person A) comments about how person B) speaks too loud.

-A) "Stop speaking so loudly, it sounds as though you are shouting and it quickly becomes tiring."

-B) "I'm not sure I understand? You are saying that I speak very loud all the time?"

-A) "Well, not always, but sometimes you do. Especially when you are with a group of people."

-B) "OK, I see. I will think about it and see if I can do something about it. Are there any other habits of mine which you think may cause a problem?"

ASSERTIVENESS TRAINING

As you can see, the negative inquiry encourages the person that is directing criticism at you to become assertive in their responses, which is more likely to create an opportunity that leads to a healthier form of communication. If person B would have responded with something defensive such as "Well you tend to speak loudly often too", the conversation could have quickly turned sour.

The basics remain the same: Avoid reacting to the criticism by being defensive and instead try to keep calm and be receptive. Don't answer by throwing criticisms of your own or by acting defensive. And avoid being sarcastic with your responses, as you want to convey a message of openness/genuine interest and sarcasm does precisely the opposite.

When you find yourself in a situation that could develop into conflict, or you're already dealing with a challenging scenario, try these techniques and see how well they work for you.

In some cases, some will work better than others, so it is up to you to find which works best in specific situations. When done sincerely, you'll find that they will help you stay away from conflict, and in many cases, even help reverse the hostility, which opens the door to have more constructive conversations later.

Remaining assertive in most situations, especially in the face of aggression or manipulation, sends a clear message: that you're not manipulable. And if the person you're communicating with doesn't like that fact, he's free to find someone else that they feel more comfortable interacting.

CHAPTER 8: ASSERTIVENESS IS A CHOICE

As mentioned earlier, it's pervasive to think that confidence or assertiveness as something that you're either born with or without. If you're born with it, you're lucky that you're destined to go throughout life with your chest puffed up and accomplishing most of what you set yourself to do. Or if you're unlucky enough to be born without it, you're pretty much destined to be a wallflower with little sense of self-worth.

Every single day we make several small subconscious choices that accomplish one of two things: they either help us by asserting our ideas or hinder us because we avoid making our needs and opinions known to the world.

People that tend to use a passive communication style seem to find it easier to go with the flow and avoid potential conflict at all costs. But as you know by now, not being assertive will only increase negative feelings such as frustration, anxiety, and guilt.

A lot of our everyday habits, even the ones that may appear insignificant, contribute to our sense of assertiveness and confidence or feelings of self-worth. We might not be aware that specific behavior patterns are affecting our sense of personal conviction, when in reality they are. Let's take a look at some of the most common habits that impact our sense of self-worth negatively:

Not having clear boundaries

Whenever we interact with others, whether it is friends, colleagues, or family members, boundaries are essential to get others to respect your needs, time and space.

If you already have very clearly defined boundaries, then great. But if that is not the case, you'll find that the lack of respect will quickly start to bring you down.

Whenever you let others affect your time, (for instance, when you're pulled from doing something important against your will to do something for someone), your sense of self-worth diminishes. The same happens whenever you say yes to something that you, in reality, didn't want to do. Placing clear boundaries may be tough, because of how most of us are taught from an early age to be nice, but letting people affect your time and space will cause you a lot of harm.

Being your own worst critic

We all tend to talk to ourselves throughout the day, and this self-talk can either help you or hinder your sense of confidence and self-worth.

It's crucial to be aware of any unfair or harsh judgments that may be floating inside your head.

Whenever you say something to yourself such as: "I can't believe the dumb things I've said today," or "I'm never able to be on time," you are doing a big disservice to your self-esteem. Our thoughts and words matters, and the unfair criticism that is going inside our heads gradually erode our sense of self-worth.

In my case, I was probably my most brutal critic. Whenever I failed, my mind never failed to insult me for a while afterward an unfortunate event happened. It wasn't until I began meditating and realizing that we have complete control over our thoughts and minds when I finally realized that it is possible to stop these negative patterns from gaining momentum.

Catching this unfair criticism and giving yourself a break is crucial.

It's especially useful to replace this unfair self-judgment with something more positive. Instead of saying to yourself, "I said stupid stuff at the meeting today," say, "I will try to be better prepared so that I can say better things next time."

Judging others

Just as it is not helpful to be your harsh judge, passing judgment on others will also affect your feelings of confidence and self-worth. Judging others means that you're allying with negativity, which will inevitably make you feel bad in the end.

Instead, try thinking good thoughts whenever possible so that you can spread some positivity around. If you need to make a criticism, make sure that you are doing it from a place of respect and a genuine desire to help others improve.

Having poor body language and not being aware of it

As you already know, the type of body language that you use daily has a massive impact on the way that you feel mentally. Because of this, we must become aware of the type of body language that we are using. Ask yourself if you are using the right posture for the situation, if you are looking at people in the eye when talking to them, whether you're fidgeting with your hands or hair, etc.

By using powerful and confident body language such as standing straight and pushing your shoulders, you will automatically feel more confident and self-worthy.

Eliminating toxic relationships

The people that you choose to often interact with will have a significant impact on whether you feel good about yourself or not. We've all heard how we are deeply influenced by the type of people that we most often surround ourselves, and it is 100% true: if you tend to keep a lot of toxic people close to you, their actions will end up having a profound influence on your sense of confidence and self-worth.

Toxic relationships zap us of our energy and exhaust us even beyond the time that we spend interacting with them. You will waste a lot of time trying to figure them out and will also feel guilty whenever you think about them as being difficult people.

The best thing you can do is to remove these kinds of people from your life as soon as possible.

Try to identify which are the most toxic influences on your life that don't bring anything positive to the table. Once you "detox" your life from negative people, you'll have a lot more time to spend on essential matters, have more energy and a better sense of self-worth.

Playing it safe

Have you ever taken a risk and it paid off in the end? It probably felt great and made you feel empowered. While I don't recommend you to put yourself in dangerous situations, you should try to take occasional risky moves whenever you think that it might have a positive impact in the most critical areas of your life, such as your career.

It may sound counterintuitive, but playing it safe and never experiencing failure may not do much for our sense of self-worth. Not taking risks sends a compelling message to our minds: that we can't handle challenging situations since we aren't able to handle mess-ups.

The more you can handle rejections and failures, the more you'll feel confident and reliant on your abilities and knowledge.

Failing to say what you're thinking

There are a time and place for everything, and we shouldn't be rude or say whatever pops in our heads just because we want to, but there is a lot to lose when we fail to speak our minds when interacting with others.

It may feel uncomfortable since you are exposing yourself to interruptions or to be talked over, but we are doing a massive disservice to our sense of self-worth whenever we think that what others have to say is more important than what we do.

Comparing ourselves to others

Have you ever seen a TV show and thought "How I wish that I had the same life as X celebrity"? Nowadays, especially with the ever-growing presence of social media in our daily lives, it can be very easy to be constantly comparing ourselves with others.

Whenever you feel bad about yourself because of your imaginary perception of another person's life, you are experiencing negativity. The same thing happens when you compare your life with those of other's to make yourself feel better.

Because of this, it's essential to stay in tune with our thoughts and catch ourselves whenever we find our minds measuring the lives of others against ours.

Now, it's a very different thing to look up to certain people as a source of inspiration to improve your life. It is recommended to look up to people that have certain traits that you wish you had. Having mentors and role models can be incredibly useful. You can use them as motivation and role models and imitate their positive behaviors so that you get to where you want quicker.

Having unrealistic expectations of yourself

Achieving goals is one of the most powerful things we can do to boost our sense of self-worth. However, goal setting can easily backfire: if we give ourselves highly ambitious and unrealistic goals, we will set ourselves to failure and disappointment. For instance, if you were interested in losing some weight, and you set a goal of losing 30 pounds in the first month, you'll probably feel pretty deflated when you don't reach your objective.

The best thing to do is to set up short term goals that can help you taste the satisfaction of constant achievement so that you feel motivated to continue moving forward.

Using your past experiences incorrectly

Confident people spend little time dwelling on the past and tend to be continually looking for what's next. They know that it's essential to learn from past errors, but don't fall into the trap of reflecting on what happened over and over again.

Whenever we dwell on our past failures and let them dictate our decisions for us, we spend time feeling a sense of failure, regret, or inadequacy that will end up hindering us.

Instead of dwelling on your past mistakes, use them as an opportunity to change things that you are dissatisfied with your current lifestyle.

Not going after the things you want

Whenever there's something that you wish to go after, a sense of desire is sparked, and not following through on it will negatively affect your sense of accomplishment and thus your self-worth.

Not taking action on what we want is one of the biggest confidence killers out there. Real confidence comes quicker when we do things that we are unfamiliar with over and over again, and our self-esteem is fed from feeling that we are worthy enough to deserve what you want in life.

Healthy habits for our self-esteem

Now that we are aware of some of the most damaging practices out there for our sense of self-worth and confidence, let's explore some of the positive things you can do every day to start believing more and more in your abilities.

-Being transparent and genuine

If you're not used to expressing yourself honestly and transparently, you will probably find it difficult at first, but once you get the ball rolling, it will feel as though a significant weight has been lifted from your life.

Can you think about the times that you've hidden behind a false smile instead of saying what we believe genuinely to feel resentful or angry afterward?

Being able to express yourself honestly takes practice, but once you get this habit incorporated into your life, people will be more open to hearing from you, and you'll feel much more confident.

-Be aware of your strengths

Think of all the times that someone has complimented you or given positive feedback about something you did. Think about how you were able to contribute to a situation and make it better. Try to think about the tasks you like and dislike. Whenever we have a success, it's important to latch onto it and replay it again and again in our minds. Keeping in mind, positive feedback from others will help us be aware of our strengths and internalize them. Savoring positive feedback can do wonders to your sense of self-worth.

ASSERTIVENESS TRAINING

-Accept when there are differences

Being assertive means that you respect your point of view as much as you appreciate others'. Just as you state your thoughts and opinions, you need to work to understand the point of view of others.

There will often be differences, and it's important not to allow them to affect us negatively. Remember that having differences doesn't necessarily mean that someone is right and someone wrong. Strive to understand the point of view of others by listening with respect and without interrupting them.

When you're practicing being assertive, it's crucial to speak in a way that doesn't make others feel guilty. Speaking up and letting others know what you think shouldn't make others feel wrong.

ASSERTIVENESS TRAINING

-Take small steps if you're struggling

Practicing being assertive can be especially tricky for those that have years of passive or aggressive habits ingrained. If you find that you're having a hard time practicing an assertive communication style, don't be afraid to take tiny steps. You could even start by making simple adjustments such as making sure that you maintain eye contact properly whenever you talk with someone or check that you have your shoulders back whenever you're walking. Even these small efforts will help you feel more assertive and confident.

After a while, you can use the confidence you've built up when interacting with others. For instance, if someone cut in front of you at the bank, be polite, and ask them to move back. If you're not satisfied with a product or service that you've paid for, try to get a refund or get to an agreement with the seller.

ASSERTIVENESS TRAINING

-Avoid slipping into passive-aggressive behavior

When you're practicing assertiveness, you'll probably feel tempted at certain times to slip into a passive-aggressive mode. You may feel like you're assertive, but in reality you're not. And it does nothing to feed your healthy sense of self-worth in the long run. For instance, say that you've been annoyed by the fact that your roommate never washes his dishes. You might have thought that making snide passive-aggressive comments is the easiest thing to do, but it's best to act deliberately instead. Tell the person what you're feeling or thinking without resorting to accusatory comments. Say your concerns in a clear and straightforward fashion. And don't forget to follow up with a suggestion on how the person can correct the situation. Using the same example, you could tell your roommate: "If you checked the sink to see if there aren't any dirty dishes of yours at least once per day, that would be a big help."

ASSERTIVENESS TRAINING

-Fake it until you make it

You won't be able to become more assertive and confident in a couple of days or weeks. It takes time and consistent practice to become a person that can stand up for what he thinks while having the respect of others. While you find yourself practicing in the beginning stages, you might feel like you are not yourself, since you're starting to implement several changes when interacting with others and that may not feel natural. Remember that being assertive has nothing to do with changing your core self. It's all about setting boundaries, standing up to what you believe and being respected by others while respecting their rights.

While you find yourself in those beginning learning stages, it might help you if you think that you're an actor that is playing a role. Imagine the most assertive person you can think of, in real life or from fiction.

ASSERTIVENESS TRAINING

Whenever you're about to handle a situation that requires you to be assertive or confident, think about how that person would feel the same situation.

Conclusion

After practicing some of the principles in this guide for a while, it won't take long for you to notice that choosing to be assertive requires a great deal of effort and commitment. It will not always be smooth sailing, especially at first when there's an initial period of discomfort for not only you but those that you interact with as you'll probably have a hard time finding the right balance between passiveness and aggressiveness. Because of this, you'll notice how the way you interact with others, and the way other people treat you will change.

Those closest to you will probably have the hardest time accepting the new and improved version of yourself. It's hard to blame them; after all, they've seen you behave a certain way for a long time, so don't expect them to treat you differently immediately.

In some cases, even expect a certain degree of resistance.

It took me a while, but eventually, even those closest to me started treating me differently, in a positive way. I'm now known as the guy that loves to speak up his mind and am even asked by others to help them with socially challenging situations. Instead of feeling fearful or anxious, I now find it pleasurable when dealing with these kinds of interactions.

If you ever feel discouraged, it is essential to remind yourself that you are choosing to operate from a position of equality and not selfishness. With constant practice, you'll become better calibrated, and others will feel more comfortable and appreciated in your presence.

Becoming more assertive is like riding a bicycle without falling, and through practice, you'll eventually find the right balance to keep you going.

It likely won't happen overnight, but by applying the strategies and advice in this guide, you'll start to build up confidence, healthier self-esteem and will inevitably become more productive, efficient, and respected by others.

Thank you, and good luck!

About the Author

Zac Cruz is a personal development author and musician who is on a mission to empower people to harness their infinite potential so they can pave the way to positive transformation in all areas of their lives. With first-hand experience of what intense shyness, bad habits, and lack of organization can do to one's overall confidence and quality of life, he ultimately took matters into his own hands and turned his life around. Going from timid to tenacious and from stagnant to flexible, he truly understands every challenge one faces along the way and has made it his lifelong purpose to help others step into their best versions.

CPSIA information can be obtained
at www.ICGtesting.com
Printed in the USA
BVHW040944311019
562588BV00006B/34/P